HELPING
VICTIMS OF
SEXUAL
ABUSE

HELPING VICTIMS OF SEXUAL ABUSE

Lynn Heitritter & Jeanette Vought

BETHANY HOUSE PUBLISHERS
MINNEAPOLIS, MINNESOTA 55438
A Ministry of Bethany Fellowship, Inc.

Published by Bethany House Publishers
A Division of Bethany Fellowship, Inc.
6820 Auto Club Road, Minneapolis, Minnesota 55438

Printed in the United States of America

Library of Congress Cataloging-in-Publication Data

Heitritter, Lynn.
   Helping victims of sexual abuse / Lynn Heitritter and Jeanette Vought.
     p.   cm.
   Bibliography: p.
   Includes index.

   1. Sexually abused children—Pastoral counseling of.
2. Adult child sexual abuse victims—Patoral counseling of.
I. Vought, Jeanette. II. Title.
BV4464.3.H44   1989
261.8'32—dc20   89-15153
ISBN 0-87123-930-2   CIP

We wish to acknowledge our families for their unfailing support, encouragement, and prayer during the preparation of this work. We thank you and we love you.

We wish to dedicate this book to the courageous women and men who have "fought the good fight" into recovery and shared their lives with us so that together, we might encourage others to come out of the darkness into the Light.

LYNN HEITRITTER, RN, BS, has been a licensed foster parent to physically and sexually abused children. She is the author of *Little Ones Activity Workbook: Protecting Your Child from Sexual Assault*, founder/former director of the BECOMERS Sexual Abuse Support Group Program. She is a seminar leader in Breaking the Silence seminars through the ministry of Damascus, Inc., and a workshop presenter equipping clergy and laypersons in acquiring skills to break cycles of shame in family systems and church systems. She also conducts family wellness seminars, is a trained Myers-Briggs Type Indicator practicioner, and holds her Parent Educator/Family Education license in the state of Minnesota. She is currently pursuing her Ph.D. in Family Social Science at the University of Minnesota. She and her husband make their home in Minneapolis, Minnesota with their two teenage daughters.

JEANETTE VOUGHT is the founder and Executive Director of the Christian Recovery Center, a ministry that specializes in issues of emotional, physical, and sexual abuse recovery. The Christian Recovery Center is committed to providing consultation and training services and to the development of abuse recovery groups across the country. She was formerly Executive Director of the New Life Family Services for twelve years, and is also the author of *Post Abortion Trauma* (Zondervan, 1991). Jeanette holds a Ph.D. in Counseling Psychology, is a professional Psychologist, a Licensed Marriage and Family Therapist, and a Clinical Social Worker. Her family includes four grown sons. She and her husband live in Minneapolis, Minnesota.

Anyone wishing to contact the authors to schedule training seminars and workshops, to request BECOMERS "start-up" packets or additional resources, or for assistance in developing a local BECOMERS group may contact them at the following address:

> % BECOMERS
> Christian Recovery Center
> 3735 North Lakeland Avenue, Suite 120
> Minneapolis, MN 55422
> (612)588–2505

To the Reader

Sexual abuse is not only prevalent in society at large but is occurring within the church as well. Many people within our churches secretly bear the scars of childhood abuse and desperately struggle with hidden trauma that interferes with spiritual growth and relationships with others. In recent years, we have come to recognize the need to inform the church about sexual abuse, as well as to provide specific materials that would enable the church to deal effectively with victims of this abuse. This book has been written for that purpose: to equip members of the body of Christ to help men and women who have been victims of sexual abuse.

Our purpose is threefold. First, we hope to provide the Christian counselor and clergy with a better understanding of the experience of sexual abuse victims and to give the counselor material to be used as a tool in the recovery process of victims and their families.

Second, we want to help victims understand some of the effects of their sexual abuse, see the need to participate in their own recovery, and be encouraged to know that many victims have recovered and gone on to live satisfying and successful lives.

Third, we wish to help friends, relatives, and spouses in their efforts to be supportive to loved ones who have been victims of sexual abuse.

Each of the three sections of this book presents a particular focus. The first acquaints the reader with sexual abuse as seen through the eyes of a child, including life histories of victims sharing the trauma of their childhood experiences. Special attention is given to the impact of abuse on the child victim. This section also describes the physical, emotional, psychological, and spiritual damage of sexual abuse.

Section two gives an overview of sexual abuse within the family, with treatment goals for intervention in the incestuous family system. This section concludes with psychological and spiritual influences in the lives of sexual abuse offenders. A description of different types of offenders is presented with treatment issues that need to be addressed.

The third section of this book presents the BECOMERS Sexual Abuse program, with instructions for starting sexual abuse support groups. Teaching materials, illustrations, and individual homework questions are included.

This book is the result of over twenty years collective experience of the authors and over two years of research and preparation. To the fullest extent of our knowledge, we have given credit to all the authors and other sources of materials that have been used in our research and writing. We appreciate each of these contributions to our work.

We have written out of deep concern for victims within churches across the nation crying out for help, looking to lay persons, Christian counselors, and the clergy in an effort to find someone to meet their needs. Our prayer is that God will use this book, in combination with members of His church through the power of the Holy Spirit, to bring restoration and healing.

Contents

Section One

Understanding the Abused Child

◇ **1** ◇

Messages . . .

They cry in the dark so you can't see their tears
They hide in the light so you can't see their fears.
Forgive and forget all the while . . .
Love and pain
Become one and the same
In the eyes of a wounded child. . . .[1]

We all receive "messages" in childhood that have an effect on our adult life, messages transmitted to us primarily through relationships with others. These early transmissions have a powerful influence on our concept of being loved, being valuable, and belonging.

The messages received by children who are sexually abused have a devastating impact on them. Some sources indicate that every two minutes in the United States a child is sexually abused, but that less than 2% of molestations are ever reported. The following life histories give us a glimpse of the messages abused children received.

Parental Incest

Julie's Messages

Grown-ups had told Julie that as a baby she was her father's pride and joy—his little red-headed sweetheart. But while still a preschooler, she began to feel the negative effects of his presence. At the end of the day, he would pick her up and rub his

---

[1]Benatar, Pat, "Hell is for Children," *Live From Earth*, (N.Y.: Chrysalis Records, Inc.).

bristly beard on her soft face and demand, "How about a kiss for your dad who's been working hard all day?" As his burly strength trespassed the boundaries of her shyness and her fear, she began to "hear" a nonverbal message: *His feelings are more important than mine.*

Vague uneasiness grew into fear as Julie and her brother experienced her father's unpredictable and explosive anger. Her mother's form of discipline was the continual threat, "You just wait till your father gets home!" Beatings with a belt that left bloody stripes on her frail body and having to lie at school about the facial bruises and black eyes were enough to convince Julie: *I am a worthless and unlovable kid.*

She cowered in her room one night, writhing in emotional pain as she heard her brother screaming during a beating. Frozen in fear, she raged with hate for her father—yet he was her security. She knew children were supposed to love their parents, and this strangling hatred printed an indelible message in her mind: *I am bad because I hate my father.*

One evening just before her mother went out, she asked 9-year-old Julie to shower before going to bed. About half an hour later her father sent her brother to bed and suggested that because he, too, needed to take a shower, they should shower together to save water. Feeling acutely embarrassed, Julie replied she'd rather shower alone. Her father's suggestion soon became a command and he pulled her into the bathroom. Her stomach knotted with fear and her heart pounded furiously as he ordered her to undress. He "explained" how stupid she was for feeling embarrassed. After all, she was "his little girl." He had changed her diapers and had seen her undressed for years; in fact, until she died he would have that right! Julie wished she could crawl into the wall to escape his prying eyes.

Then he approached her in an unusually nurturing way and began to fondle her as he explained "where babies come from." He seemed to be actually caring for her!

A volcano of conflicting feelings erupted all at once. Her enjoyment of some physical pleasure and this new-found closeness with her father clashed violently with the disgust, shame, and fear at what was happening to her. She felt dizzy.

When she passed out from the intensity of the physical and emotional distress, a new message was recorded: *Bad love is better than no love at all.*

Julie's experience is not unusual. One-fifth of all American families are involved in some form of child abuse,[2] and leading authorities believe 1 in 10 families is involved in incestuous abuse. Researchers estimate for every case of incest that is reported, at least 25 cases remain hidden.[3] In the United States, the average incest victim is 11 years old, although some victims are infants and some are in their late teens. The child is usually approached sexually in early childhood between ages 5 to 8. Infrequently, a single act of incest occurs that is not repeated, but most commonly, the incest continues for 3 to 5 years or longer.[4] While accurate statistics on incest are impossible to compile due to the many unreported cases, the problem is much more prevalent than most of us would care to admit.

Julie's father was not some sort of freakish pervert. Like many men who abuse their children, he was a well-respected, wealthy member of his community, and, in this case, a deacon in his church as well. The church can no longer ignore the possibility that sexual abuse exists behind its own doors.

Neighborhood Molestation

Laurie's Messages

When Laurie was 9, her mom and dad divorced. Her mother was so grieved and hurt over the divorce that she didn't have time for Laurie and the other children. This lack of care and attention communicated clearly to Laurie: *If people I care about reject me, I must be unlovable.*

To fill this empty place, Laurie started spending more time away from home with a new friend, a 39-year-old man named Joe. Because Joe worked with cars as her father had done, his companionship brought back memories of the few special times she had enjoyed with her father at his auto body shop.

---

[2]Carole Allen-Baley, "For Kids' and Parents' Sake," *World Vision* (May 1983), 11.

[3]Adele Mayer, *Sexual Abuse: Causes, Consequences and Treatment of Incestuous and Pedophilic Acts* (Holmes Beach, Calif.: Learning Publications, Inc., 1985), 6.

[4]Linda Tschirhart Sanford, *The Silent Children: A Parent's Guide to the Prevention of Child Sexual Abuse* (New York: McGraw-Hill, 1982), 154.

Joe was like a father to her. He took her everywhere with him, bought her gifts, and gave her anything that she wanted. It all seemed too good to be true. He told her she was his girl, and that their relationship would always be special. She gladly gave him the hugs he asked for and enjoyed being cuddled on his lap. For the first time she could remember, she was loved.

She spent more and more time at Joe's home—it was her favorite place to be. One afternoon, however, while she was sitting on Joe's lap as they watched TV, he starting fondling her. She became uneasy and scared. She wanted to be loved, to be special to someone, to have nice things as the other girls had, but something was going wrong. This was her best friend, but his touching didn't feel good. She tried to move away from him, but his grip remained firm.

As he continued, confusion overwhelmed her. He had been so good to her and had given her so many things. He loved her. Surely he wouldn't do anything bad. After all, she was the unlovable one. The message became firmly imprinted in her mind: *I must be dependent on others; they are wiser and stronger than I am*. At the age of 9, she was convinced that she was so worthless that she must let others decide what was best for her, even if she didn't like it.

This was just the beginning of Laurie's nightmare of sexual abuse. Though she was fearful and confused, her desperate need for love drove her deeper into dependence upon Joe. She continued going to his house, even though his actions became increasingly bizarre. She felt like two persons—one willingly participating in the abuse, the other filled with shame and fear. It seemed as if she were standing outside of herself watching this happen to someone else.

Gradually Joe led her into all kinds of sexual perversion, robbing her childhood innocence. Hating who she was and what had happened to her, she turned away from God and her family, drinking to numb the gnawing pain within and using drugs to forget the awful things that had happened. Finally, at age 13, Laurie could take no more. She ran away from home. Alone, frightened, deeply wounded, and chemically dependent, she began working the streets of Minneapolis as a prostitute. It was the only way she knew to take care of herself and try to be loved.

Abuse like Laurie's is all too prevalent, and produces predictable results. In a study of 118 female chemical abusers, 44% were victims of incest and 75% reported having been sexually abused before the age of 9.[5] Another study of 200 street prostitutes documented that 75% of them had been raped as children.[6]

Sexual abuse is one of the three main reasons children run away from home.[7] While Laurie's story may seem like an extreme case, the progression from sexual abuse to chemical dependency and prostitution is tragically common. Even in cases where the victim does not engage in prostitution, many women still "prostitute" themselves by trading sexual promiscuity in exchange for someone to care.

In the United States today, a child rape occurs once every 45 minutes.[8] In Laurie's case, and in countless others, the offender did not need to use physical force. Instead, the child was manipulated with gifts and affection as the offender built a trusting relationship with the child, then sexually exploited her. For every victim of incest, an estimated 10 young victims are molested by an offender outside the family.[9] The sad fact of Laurie's story is that most such cases are never reported because the victim feels guilty and ashamed, and intensely fears rejection and abandonment.

Pedophile Abuse

Jim's Messages

When his father died, Jim was 2 months old, the youngest of three children. His mother soon began to work full time, and from about age 2, he was cared for by babysitters. The lack of a nurturing relationship with his mother and the absence of a father's care left Jim with strong feelings of insecurity and emptiness.

Because Jim's older brother was very rebellious and caused his mother many problems, Jim began early to hear the message: *If I am good, I will be loved.* Even though he resented the amount

---

[5]J. Densen-Gerber, "The Big Issue," *Odyssey House* (July 1977).
[6]T. Elias, "Young Female Prostitutes," *The Press*, vol. 10, #5 (October 1982).
[7]Mayer, *Sexual Abuse*, 7.
[8]Sanford, *The Silent Children*, 8.
[9]David Finkelhor, "A Hidden Epidemic," *Newsweek* (May 1984).

of attention his older brother received because of his misbehavior, Jim continued striving to be the "good boy" Mom wanted. Feeling responsible to try to make his mother's life easier, he set aside his own needs for love and acceptance. A new message was taking root: *I am responsible for the behavior and feelings of those around me.*

When Jim was 11, his mother married a university professor, a charming and handsome man with a Ph.D. in psychology. But Jim had difficulty trusting this stranger who had become "father," because soon after their marriage the couple began to argue frequently. Jim had already been sensitized to think that he was responsible for the way others felt, but another message was coming through: *I am responsible to bring about change when I see it is needed.* He felt he should try to get along with his stepfather; maybe by being extra "good" he could help his mother's situation.

Jim's stepfather liked to hunt and fish, and he began spending a great deal of time with Jim, seeming to show genuine care. The stepfather told Jim that his mother was the cause of all the problems in the marriage, thus planting seeds of insecurity within Jim about his mother's care for him. When his mother would discipline him, Jim's stepfather would use the incident to prove to Jim that his mother did not understand or love him. While the stepfather was sabotaging the relationships between Jim, his mother, and his siblings, this man acted as a "pal" to him. Jim, the compassionate rescuer of the underdog, had long since learned the message: *I need other people's approval in order to be happy.* In this sensitive boy's mind, the stepfather painted a picture of himself as a poor, beleaguered man whom Jim should feel sorry for.

Feeling alienated from his mother and family, Jim's mind recorded a new message: *I must be independent because others are untrustworthy.* Feeling alone and rejected, he put up a wall against people. In spite of his resolve not to trust anyone, however, he began to depend increasingly on his stepfather for the care and acceptance he needed. The groundwork had been laid. It was a very short step from this betrayal of Jim's innocence to sexual exploitation.

During a particularly difficult time, when his stepfather was sobbing, saying he would have to leave home, he threw himself on 11-year-old Jim, crying and hugging him. Jim felt sorry for him and tried his best to comfort him. In the days following, the hugging became more frequent and more sustained, until his stepfather began kissing him. Acutely embarrassed and ashamed, Jim felt this was wrong and was deeply confused but had no one to talk to.

When they went hunting together and had to sleep in the same bed, Jim awoke to overt sexual advances by his stepfather. This was the only significant relationship he had in his life, but it was growing into something dirty and scary. Jim felt the suffocating oppression of being absorbed by his stepfather, losing his identity. He couldn't bring himself to talk about it; he was certain that no one would believe him, that he was a total "jerk," and he was terribly ashamed and guilty, like a woman who had been raped. He was being destroyed, used up, and there was no place to hide.

What happened to Jim happens to thousands of young boys across America each year. It is reported that 9% of American men were sexually abused as children.[10] Statistics vary from reports that 1 out of every 6 boys will be sexually misused before high school,[11] to reports that 1 out of every 8 males will be abused before the age of 18.[12] Because compiling accurate statistics is difficult, the problem is likely underestimated.

While most victims of incest are females (7 out of 8 incest reports will involve a female victim), most victims of pedophiles are preadolescent boys about ages 8 to 10.[13] A pedophile, an adult sexually attracted to children, most often preys upon young boys lacking a father figure. These boys, starved for male attention and love, will often feel a deep sense of loyalty toward this type of offender and not report the abuse. According to the FBI, pedophiles themselves claim that 20 million American men are sexually attracted to boys alone.[14] A study of 1,000 pedophiles showed that less than 1% of those arrested were incarcerated.[15]

---

[10]Allen-Baley, "For Kids' and Parents' Sake," 11.

[11]World Vision Magazine, May 1983, 11.

[12]R.L. Geiser, *Hidden Victims: The Sexual Abuse of Children* (Boston, Mass.: Beacon Press, 1979), 46.

[13]Mayer, *Sexual Abuse*, 8.

[14]Kenneth V. Lanning, "Child Protection Alert," *FBI Law Enforcement Bulletin* (January 1984), 10.

[15]Geiser, *Hidden Victims*, 8.

Researchers believe that 75% of parents who have some reason to believe their child was molested do not report it.[16] What is unusual, in Jim's case, is that the offender actually married Jim's mother in order to have access to him, and the abuse continued for years without intervention.

Sibling Incest

Diane's Messages

When Diane was born, her mother was overwhelmed by the birth of this sixth child and went into a severe depression for over a year. The younger children were passed around from relative to relative and, as a result, felt they didn't belong anywhere. When Diane's mom came back to the family after a lengthy hospital stay for depression, she was functional but unable to interact emotionally with her children. Diane's father was a cold and distant person, punishing his children with stony silence and cruel indifference.

Diane tried desperately to earn her parents' approval by being good and by always controlling and "stuffing" her feelings. Whenever she expressed anger, her parents withdrew from her and she felt rejected. She soon internalized the message: *I am bad if I feel angry.* There was no hugging or demonstration of affection between Diane's parents or between the parents and the children. The children were often left in the care of their older brother, who was aggressive and demanding. Diane soon learned that resisting her older brother's rules brought hostile punishing silence from her parents, so she began to believe a new message: *I must keep the peace at any price.*

When she was 6 years old, her brother approached her with a "game" that he insisted would be fun, so she allowed him to fondle her, teaching her to manipulate herself to "feel good." To Diane it seemed fairly harmless; it was their "secret." After all, it was the only time her brother had treated her nicely or that anyone had paid any attention to her.

The game continued with increasing frequency, and her brother began to demand more sexual involvement. On the farm

---

[16]Ibid., 7.

where they lived there were many isolated places available. He forced her to cooperate with his games, threatening to tell their mother that Diane had been "fooling around with herself" and that she had taken her clothes off and crawled into bed with him. What could she say? Those things were true—but not as he made them out to be.

Frustrated, alone, with nowhere to turn, Diane continued as her brother's passive partner in the sex play. Thinking she was *trapped and could never change,* she suppressed the sense of humiliation and disgust for her brother, while maintaining her act of passive accommodation. She tried not to think about the problem, hoping that if she ignored it, it would go away. A sense of inferiority overwhelmed her.

She compared herself to the other girls at school and felt they knew something was wrong with her, so she painfully strove to achieve perfection, hoping flawless performance would cover up the nagging guilt and shame within her. The fear of making a mistake nearly paralyzed her, for *mistakes only confirmed her worthlessness.*

The perverted relationship with her brother, coupled with her cold and distant father, distorted her view of men and she became intensely anxious around any man. Compounding the blurring of roles were the sermons she heard in church about God being a loving heavenly Father. What had she done to cause these things to happen to her? Maybe God was punishing her for being bad, and that was why her brother kept hurting her. Perhaps she had seduced her brother after all. Maybe what he said about her was true.

She took measures to protect herself. Her brother once remarked that she had pretty hair, so she cut it, thinking short hair would be safer. She began eating to comfort her pain and calm her anxieties and gained 80 pounds. She wore boys' clothing. She built walls of silence, withdrawal, and isolation, spending many hours in her room alone. At age 10, she made a solemn vow: *No one would ever get close enough to hurt her again.*

Some experts estimate that casual sibling sexual contact occurs in 9 out of 10 families with more than one child. This can simply be developmental curiosity about the body parts of the opposite sex. Sibling incest is, however, quite a different issue. One author notes that sibling incest is the most widespread form of incest, though it often goes unreported, even when discovered.[17]

Neither these children nor other child victims are exempt from having some residual effects of sexual abuse on their concepts of being loved and valuable. As one victim, now an adult, stated, "When somebody sexually abuses you, they don't just invade your body . . . they invade your soul." The entire person is touched by the trauma: physically, emotionally, intellectually, psychologically, and spiritually.

Glimpses into the lives of these four children show that the messages received from each abusive situation had a profound and destructive impact. These children believed these messages to be true about who they were and about their value as a person. They will continue to live their lives based on those messages and most likely will pass them on to others . . . unless someone intervenes.

---

[17]Susan Forward and Craig Buck, *Betrayal of Innocence: Incest and Its Devastation* (Jeremy P. Tarcher, Inc., Los Angeles), 85.

◇ 2 ◇

Through the Eyes of a Child Victim

As we discuss issues of abuse, the child is referred to as a "victim" because children are always victimized by sexual abuse, even when they are willing participants in the sexual behavior. Children lack the emotional and intellectual ability to withstand premature introduction of sexuality by an adult. Many offenders will rationalize their offense by stating that a child was trying to "turn them on" when, in fact, the child was displaying age-appropriate exploratory or acting-out behavior. The appropriate adult response to such behavior in a child would be to set limits or redirect the child's behavior.

Children are victims because they are exploited by the offender's abuse of power. This misuse of power can victimize the child through force or threats of physical power and/or the manipulation or intimidation of abusive emotional power. The offender has the resource of knowing that the behavior is sexual in intent, while the child is victimized by the lack of that knowledge.

The Impact of Abuse

The children are victimized not only by the betrayal of their vulnerability, but also because they have no resource or reference against which to evaluate and understand the impact of the abuse. The impact on the child victim reaches into all corners of his or her being.

Confusion

Surprise and confusion are initial reactions of victims of sexual abuse. The child questions, "What is going on?" "What is happening to me?" "Is this right or wrong?" "Will it happen again?" "Should I tell someone?" Child victims experience great conflict about the many emotions they feel. Some emotions may seem pleasant, due to the closeness and/or special attention from the offender. Other emotions, such as guilt, fear, anger, and shame, are unpleasant and often frightening. This emotional confusion increases their vulnerability to being manipulated and used by the offender.

Many times the child thinks that the abusive behavior is normal because the offender has told them that it was "OK," but they are confused because they have been warned not to tell anyone. When Susanne's grandfather began fondling her when she was on his lap, she enjoyed being his special girl but was confused about why he was touching her "that way." His reply that all grandfathers showed their love to their granddaughters like this confused her even more. Her other grandfather never touched her like that. Didn't he really love her? Such confusion often intensifies as the child gets older, commonly around junior high age, and is usually magnified in adulthood.

Guilt

Almost universally, the victim feels responsible and guilty for the abuse. Children will believe the abuse was their fault for a variety of reasons: because they did nothing to try to stop the abuse; because the abuse was sometimes pleasurable, or because they feel special favors or rewards were received; because they feel they have done something to cause the abuse, or that they are so bad that they deserved the abuse.

One 40-year-old woman recounted this childhood experience. Her mother was sick in the hospital and she was afraid her mother might die. During one night of her mother's hospitalization, she went into her father's room for comfort and reassurance, but rather than comfort her, he sexually used her. This 9-year-old girl concluded that she had "caused" the abuse by going into his room. Thereafter, he came into her room at night. Because she was already convinced that she had caused the abuse to happen in the first place, she now felt she "deserved" to have it continue.

Child victims feel guilty for having feelings of both love and hate toward the person who abused them, and toward other family members who did not protect them. Victims are convinced of their "guilt" when other family members blame them for reporting the abuse, blame them for being "responsible" for a divorce, or blame them for "causing" the imprisonment of the offender.

One little girl was accused of causing her father's death after she told a teacher about the incest. Shortly after the father was confronted about the abuse, he became ill with cancer. The family told the young child that she "caused" the cancer by telling about the abuse and "making so much trouble."

The child will translate the overwhelming sense of blame, of worthlessness, of being "different" from everyone else and "dirty" into feelings of intense "guilt." But these are the feelings of shame, not guilt, and they can become a crippling bondage. The significant difference between shame and guilt will be addressed in Chapter 11 (pp. 145–146).

Fear

Child victims have many fears. They may fear that they have been physically damaged in some way because of the abuse. An abused teen had stopped having her menstrual periods due to extreme stress and fear. She mistook the absence of her menstrual flow as confirmation that her father's abuse had "broken" her inside. A child may fear being found out by others, or that others can tell by looking at them that they are bad. Fear of the family breaking up is an all-consuming fear that motivates many children into remaining in an abusive relationship. Fear of rejection by both the offender and the non-abusing parent can make the child feel there is no way out. The child may be intensely afraid of being hurt by the abuser, especially if the abuser has made threats. The very real danger of personal harm must not be discounted by those who become involved in abuse situations. One 13-year-old girl was threatened with death if she ever told anyone that her father was abusing her. The father was later picked up on abuse charges for abusing another young girl. At the trial, his daughter testified against him to confirm the other victim's case, and he was found guilty and sent to jail.

After the trial, the daughter felt safe from him for the first time in her life. But a few weeks later, a car deliberately tried to run her down as she was walking home. She was able to jump out of the way, and she found out later that her father had actually hired someone to kill her. She left the state to live with relatives, but continued to live with tremendous fear.

Anger

Child victims usually experience great anger but have no outlet of expression. They feel angry at what the abuser has done. They may feel angry at themselves for not trying to stop the abuse, or for enjoying parts of the abusive relationship. The child victim is often angry at the non-abusing parent for not being protective or for not stopping the abuse. The child may outwardly appear passive or compliant, but inwardly may be seething with resentment and hostility. Eph. 6:4 (KJV) instructs fathers to "provoke not your children to wrath, but bring them up in the nurture and admonition of the Lord." To provoke to anger suggests a repeated, ongoing pattern of treatment; deep-seated anger and resentment build up and finally boil over into outward hostility.[1] While the passage is primarily dealing with parental discipline, the behavior of provoking children to anger by repeated abusive acts not only violates the first section of this verse, but violates the principle of nurture in the second section.

Philip was being sexually abused by his priest, who bribed him not to tell about their "secret." Philip's parents encouraged him to spend more and more time with their priest, and Philip grew increasingly hostile and angry. Without an outlet for this anger, Philip started torturing animals to express his rage; his parents finally sought some professional help after he drowned the family cat. The sexually abused child becomes the soil where seeds of "provoked anger" intermix with seeds of anger over lack of nurture, to create an explosive, destructive force that chokes the child's spirit.

---

[1]John F. MacArthur, *The MacArthur New Testament Commentary—Ephesians* (Chicago: Moody Bible Institute, 1986), 317.

Loss of Trust

In her book *Sexual Abuse,* Adele Mayer states, "Victims' loss of trust in authority figures is one of the most devastating effects of incest. Their parents are the first adults children learn to trust, and incest represents the ultimate betrayal of that trust."[2] Because of this violation of trust, children will often tell peers about sexual abuse occurring in their family before they will tell adults; they feel adults are untrustworthy. In cases where the abuse is perpetrated outside the family, trust in the parents as protectors may be damaged—even though the parents are unaware of the abuse. Many times the child assumes that the parents know—or should know—what is happening to them.

The erosion of trust is often tragically progressive in the life of the victim. With incest in the home, the child learns that the parents are not trustworthy. If other adults further abuse them, the child may conclude that there are no adults who are trustworthy. If this cycle of abuse continues in the victim's life, the adult victim may become unable to develop trust in anyone.

Marie was such a child. When she was between the ages of 5 and 10, she was fondled by two different male babysitters who were frequently left alone with her. During the same years, she observed her father in his bedroom masturbating while he looked through pornographic magazines. Her older brothers also observed their father's behavior, which stimulated them into becoming sexually involved with Marie.

By age 10, Marie was becoming convinced that she could not trust anyone older. As a teenager, she turned to peers for safety in relationships. She transferred the little trust that remained onto the friends she knew. Being raped by a group of boys from school, however, again reinforced that there was no one to trust.

As a young woman, Marie met a man who seemed trustworthy. She married him, and felt that she had found security for the first time in her life. But within the first year of marriage, she endured several incidents of physical and sexual abuse.

---

[2]Adele Mayer, *Sexual Abuse: Causes, Consequences and Treatment for Incestuous and Pedophilic Acts* (Holmes Beach, Fla.: Learning Publications, 1985), 54.

This man finalized the destruction of her trust, and she determined that she would never trust anyone again.

It seems logical, of course, that such life experiences would cost Marie her ability to trust. But much less dramatic trauma may bear the same fruit in a sensitive, wounded child. Those who would desire to help victims of sexual abuse will need to bear in mind that the impact of the abuse is the impact experienced by the *victim*. Impact cannot be evaluated from the point of view of the counselor, but rather must be discerned from the perspectives of the victims themselves.

Perspectives on Impact of Sexual Abuse

Those who work with abuse victims need to realize that the issues of childhood are relevant not only to the child who has just reported abuse but also to the adult victim who has just disclosed abuse from childhood. Many variables interact to determine the impact of abuse on an individual. In *The Silent Children,* therapist Linda Sanford writes: "Every victim of child sexual abuse needs sympathetic, professional intervention, even if it is just one visit to a social worker to clarify that the child is not responsible for the crime."[3] Her point is well taken. The minimum that a child needs is to be reaffirmed of his or her value by a trusted and caring person, and reassured that the responsibility for the abuse lies with the offender.

Age and Developmental Level

The child's perception of the abuse will vary according to age and understanding of sexuality. A younger child may simply be confused by being fondled by her uncle, while an older child with more of an understanding of sexuality might be more affected by knowing that being fondled is wrong, feeling not only violated, but somehow responsible for the sexual contact. The counselor needs to guard against minimizing the impact, because it seems to his or her adult logic that the abuse was "insignificant." Conversely, the counselor will need to be cautious that the impact of the abuse is not distorted by his or her

---

[3]Linda Tschirhart Sanford, *The Silent Children: A Parent's Guide to the Prevention of Child Sexual Abuse* (New York: McGraw-Hill, 1982), 138.

own reaction to the abuse, thus projecting more trauma onto the child than the child actually feels.

Child's Relationship With Offender

Usually the sexual crime committed by a stranger has less impact than the same crime committed by a trusted parent. Occasionally, the offender who began as a stranger to the child becomes a loved and trusted person in the child's eyes. Charlie was a stranger to his victim and her parents but, over a period of time, became a close friend to the child. Looking at the relationship with the offender from the child's perspective will help to evaluate the impact of abuse on a particular child.

Charlie's 8-year-old victim says, "I kept on trying to get my parents to understand that Charlie was my friend. They didn't know him, but they wanted to get him fired at his job in the school. I didn't want that because then Charlie wouldn't have any food to eat."[4]

Duration of the Abuse

Usually, the longer the abuse has continued, the greater the impact. The child who lives with continual sexual abuse will, out of necessity, develop increased defenses for emotional survival. The impact can be measured by the degree to which the child uses such defenses—such as denying the abuse; rationalizing that the abuse is appropriate because they deserve it; or fantasizing an ideal situation that denies the reality of their circumstances. The longer defenses like these are used by the child, the greater the distortion to the rational thinking process.

Sally pretended to everyone that she had the most wonderful dad in the world. They spent time together and seemed to have a happy family. She told no one, especially her mother, about the times that the father beat her into sexual submission, because he told her he would "beat up the old lady" if she didn't cooperate.

Because the abuse began when she was around 7 years old and continued throughout Sally's high school years, her defen-

---

[4]Ibid., 139.

ses distorted her reality to the point that she felt, as an adult, that the abuse had no effect on her. But in fact, she had frequent depressive suicidal thoughts, an abusive marriage, and difficulties being a good parent.

Type of Sexual Activity

Another variable in assessing the impact of abuse on the victim is related to the type of sexual activity and the amount of physical and emotional pain that was inflicted. It is often assumed that touching and fondling of the breasts and genital area is less traumatic than vaginal or rectal penetration, or oral sex. Not only is this assumption untrue, but other forms of non-touching sexual abuse can be equally devastating from the child's viewpoint. The following poem from *Secret Shame: I Am a Victim of Incest* illustrates the emotional trauma of the victim caused by the offender's penetrating stare.

Third Grade Teacher

Dear Third Grade Teacher:
You found me daydreaming today.
Usually I work real hard,
    finish on time,
    read lots of books,
    write poems that rhyme,
and act like a very good girl.
You scolded me
again
because I was dreaming.
You didn't know that
yesterday
when no one else was home,
Daddy made me lie on the couch
with all my clothes off.
He just sat in his big chair
and looked at me,
smiling a smile I can't understand.
I was ashamed,
embarrassed and afraid.

Today I couldn't remember
my "times eights,"

and I spent the April afternoon
daydreaming.
You didn't understand.[5]

Other areas of non-touching sexual abuse involve the emotional trauma caused by covert sexual messages directed toward the victim by the offender. Children can be victimized by observing openly displayed pornographic materials. They can also be impacted by offenders who deliberately expose themselves to a child while masturbating. Many have shared the humiliation and shame resulting from this type of victimization. Often, one type of abuse will set the victim up to be repeatedly victimized in other ways.

Some of the greatest impact is determined by the amount of physical force or threats to the victim while the abuse is occurring. When a child is both physically and sexually abused, the trauma is doubled. The added stress of the physical abuse may even overshadow the sexual abuse, at least for a time.

One 11-year-old victim explains, "When I was in the hospital, they were stitching up my face where he had hit me so hard. I forgot to tell them about the sex part until later. I was more worried about my cut-up face."[6]

Parental Reaction to the Abuse

More than any other variable, the reaction of the parents—or others who are important to the child—can have the greatest impact. "Experts agree that this is the single most important factor in preventing the abuse from becoming a life-destroying event."[7]

Great damage can be done if children are not believed when they first tell about the abuse. Most children are told by the offender not to tell, so the child is taking a great risk to confide in someone. If the child is living with, or emotionally close to the offender, disclosure will be even more difficult. Children often want to protect their parents from being hurt by knowing about the abuse, and so keep silent. Another fear of telling is

---

[5]Martha Janssen, *Secret Shame: I Am a Victim of Incest* (Minneapolis: Augsburg Fortress, 1991). Reprinted by permission.
[6]Sanford, *The Silent Children*, 140.
[7]Ibid., 142.

that the parent or special person will think the child is bad and reject him or her because of the abuse. In the light of these barriers, it is extremely important to believe a child who reports abuse.

Unfortunately, many children are not believed when they finally do tell, but instead are doubted, or even worse, accused of lying.

Author and Christian therapist David Peters states:

> A further example of our desperation to ignore the sexual abuse of children is the totally erroneous statement often heard: "It may not be true. After all, children lie about many things and could fantasize about having been sexually abused." Of all the cases I have investigated and seen investigated, I know of only one instance of a child lying about sexual abuse. Furthermore, every authority in the nation, as far as I am aware, reports the same conclusion. Children have neither the inclination nor the information necessary for false reporting.[8]

Tremendous damage is inflicted by parents or others who don't believe child victims when the abuse is reported. Failure to believe the child destroys trust and compounds the issues the victim will later have to resolve. Some parents have gone to great lengths to test their children's truthfulness about alleged abuse.

An adult victimized as a small child recalls such a situation from his childhood:

> My parents dragged me over to the coach's house. I was screaming and crying the whole way. He was the last person I wanted to see, but they were intent on this big confrontation. Of course he denied it—said I was trying to get him into trouble because I didn't make the team. . . . They believed him. I don't know which was more traumatic—the molestation or that scene.[9]

As unbelievable as this may seem, many children have endured the humiliation of being forced to face their abuser, who then discredits them and accuses them of lying. The ultimate

---

[8]David B. Peters, *A Betrayal of Innocence: What Everyone Should Know About Child Sexual Abuse* (Dallas, Tex.: Word Books, 1986), 21.
[9]Sanford, *The Silent Children*, 142–143.

trauma is added when parents believe the abuser at the expense of the child.

Evaluating "Truthfulness"

There are several factors that can help in evaluating the validity and accuracy of a child's story. First, the child usually will have the ability to give particular details about the abuse. These details would be information that is explicitly sexual or adult and of a nature that is beyond the child's developmental age.

Second, the child who has experienced abuse will usually exhibit some of the symptoms listed in Chapter 3, and the onset of those symptoms would coincide with the timing of the reported abuse.

Third, the child will likely demonstrate the kinds of vulnerabilities that "mark" him or her as a victim. These include little accurate sexual knowledge; lack of coping skills for protection; an absent parent or lack of a close relationship with one or both parents; previous abuse. When a child gives any indication that he or she might be experiencing abuse, the child's story needs to be treated with concern and respect until the full measure of that situation can be discerned.

How to Help an Abused Child

1. When a child discloses sexual abuse, try to remain calm. This will be difficult in light of the many feelings that will surface, but your feelings must be vented away from the child's presence. Do not overreact in front of the child.

2. Allow the child to describe, in his or her own words, what has physically happened. Do not ask questions that can be answered with yes or no, or suggest to the child what might have happened. Keep the number of persons interviewing the child to a minimum, both to protect the child from repeatedly having to expose the events of the abuse, and to protect the clarity of the details of the case, should it go to court.

3. Believe the child. Let the child describe the feelings resulting from the abuse and refrain from minimizing what has happened.

4. Assure the child that it was right to tell, and that he or she will be protected from the offender, if that is a threat. Protect the child's confidentiality against further trauma from peers or others at church, school, or the neighborhood.

5. Reassure the child repeatedly that the abuse was not his or her fault, that he or she is not to blame, and that he or she is not "bad" because the abuse happened. Reinforce that the offender is responsible for the abuse. Many times the child has a special relationship with the offender and has some positive feelings for him, so the child may defend the offender if you express intense or negative feelings about the offender.

6. Follow regular home routines. "One study showed that 25% of the parents of victims wanted to move out of their neighborhood after the sexual abuse committed by a person outside the family was discovered, while only about 11% of their children desired to move."[10]

Under normal circumstances, children do not usually like changes in the routines of daily living. When major changes, such as moving away, follow sexual abuse incidents, it appears that the abuse is bigger than the family's ability to cope with it. This could increase the impact of the abuse on such a child.

7. Preserve normal physical affection. This is crucial in helping the child reestablish trust in adults and assurance of care and acceptance. If a child objects to affection, his or her boundaries should definitely be respected. At the same time, try to help him or her work through fears about affection and closeness.

8. Provide the child, and each family member, with support and counseling. When a child stops talking about the abuse after disclosure, it is often perceived by parents and others as a sign that the issue has been resolved. Understandably, the family would like to forget about the abuse and get on with their lives, and telling a child to simply "forgive and forget" may temporarily soothe the family's pain. But if sufficient time isn't taken for the healing process, both the child and the family can be affected for life.

---

[10]Ibid., 145.

Recovery in Young Children

Suzanne Long, in *Sexual Abuse of Young Children,* writes about some of the guidelines for treating young girls who have been victims of incest. The following are some signs that the child is ready to terminate her counseling experience. (Although Long refers to the victim in the female gender in her work, male victimization is also prevalent.) With some modification, these indicators can be helpful in assessing the counseling progress of children who have experienced sexual abuse from any source.

Indicators for Termination of Therapy

- Has she dealt sufficiently with her feelings of guilt, fear, anger, confusion, and depression?
- Has she dealt specifically with the nature of the molestation, the methods of coercion, negative and positive feelings about it, secondary gains? [Author's note: Secondary gains are "benefits," such as conditional love in exchange for the abuse, peace in the home if the child goes along with the abuse, or earning rewards for sexual favors.]
- Does she feel less responsible for the sexual behavior, the storminess following disclosure, and the disruption to her family?
- Has she dealt with her anger and hostility at both her mother and the perpetrator for the molestation and the lack of protection from it?
- Does she demonstrate trust in her mother and see her as a protector (or have another trusting relationship with another significant adult)?
- Is she aware of earlier confusion between sex and affection?
- Is she able to set limits on sexual advances?
- Is she able to seek help in the event that she is approached again?
- Has she developed an increase in overall social skills?
- Has she developed outside social contacts and activities?
- Is she more age-appropriate in activity than at the beginning of treatment?

- Does she feel better about herself?
- Is she more trustful?[11]

These are some of the main areas addressed in professional counseling with young children. When the child has done the work involved in making many of the changes that are mentioned above, or has made significant progress in that direction, the child may have reached a stopping point in counseling, especially if the child has support at home from the parents.

Both the child and the parents should realize that future therapeutic intervention might be necessary at certain life stages that stir up old issues—at puberty; during dating, engagement or marriage; or bearing and raising children.

If it is necessary for the child to return to counseling at later stages in his or her life, this should be viewed as simply another step in the healing process. It does not mean that the victimized individual did not do their work or that God was not faithful in the healing process. It means that an old issue has surfaced that needs to be put into perspective with the individual's identity in Christ, a perspective that reaffirms that individual's value to God and others.

[11]Suzanne Long, et al, *Sexual Abuse of Young Children* (New York: The Guilford Press, 1986).
Additional resource:
Mary de Young, "A Conceptual Model for Judging the Truthfulness of a Young Child's Allegation of Sexual Abuse," *American Journal of Orthopsychiatry* (October 1986), 550–559.

◇ 3 ◇

Symptoms, Signals, Effects . . .

Early Childhood to Adult

The signs, symptoms, and effects of sexual abuse present themselves differently at different age levels. In early stages, these symptoms often go unnoticed or are ignored by those closest to the child. One key to early detection is looking for a cluster of symptoms that together might give a clearer picture than any one symptom by itself.

The presentation of any particular group of indicators or results of abuse is, of necessity, incomplete. The human spirit is extraordinarily gifted in its capacity to search for creative ways to survive trauma. The following pages illustrate "signals" and coping mechanisms of individual children and adults who have fought to survive.

Early Childhood Symptoms

Physical Signals

Some of the more overt physical signs of sexual abuse in a young child might be venereal disease, vaginitis, bladder infections, or pain in urinating or defecating. One church discovered that an adolescent boy working in their church nursery had systematically abused over 60 children throughout a two-year period. The symptoms of some of those children, ages 6 months to 24 months, was pain while having bowel movements. When one mother took her child to the doctor for an examination, the doctor told her the small lacerations in the rectal area were probably due to the child being constipated. When several children were discovered to have rectal enlargement or lacerations, however, the sexual abuse was brought to light.

Persistent sore throats or unexplained gagging can be a symptom of abuse, due to the high incidence of forced oral sex, especially with younger children.

Behavioral Signals

Many behavioral changes may signal the onset of abuse. A young child may have appetite changes or some changes in sleeping patterns. Nightmares can be a sign of abuse, as well as a sudden onset of fears or anxieties.

Fear

A child may fear strange men or strange situations. There may be a specific person or situation that the child fears. One young woman aged 25 told of being molested by her godfather when she was 8 years old. Thereafter, every time her parents wanted to go visit the godfather, who was a close friend of the family, she threw a temper tantrum and refused to go. She was punished by her parents for her disobedience to them, but her behavior was her signal that she had been abused.

Fears of playing alone, unprovoked crying spells or regression in one or more developmental areas, such as bed-wetting, thumb-sucking, or baby talk, can indicate the kinds of fears and stress experienced by an abused child.

Refusals

When a child resists a previously favorite activity, or refuses to be with a previously favorite person, the reason for that change should be carefully examined. Young Timmy was 7 years old. His father owned a local auto service station in rural Minnesota. Mr. Thompson, one of his regular customers, came over and asked if Timmy would like to go swimming with him and his son that evening. Timmy's face lit up. Swimming was his favorite thing to do! He ran and grabbed his suit and bounced out the door. Mr. Thompson took the boys out for pizza, then swimming, but later anally raped Timmy behind the K-Mart before taking him home.

The next week, Mr. Thompson came by and asked Timmy's

father if Timmy would like to go swimming with him again. Timmy's father recalled that when Timmy had come home the week before, he had been quiet and said he didn't have a very good time. Timmy looked at the floor and said he really didn't want to go. His well-meaning father insisted that because he liked swimming so much he should go. He assured Timmy that he would have a good time once he got there.

That evening Mr. Thompson repeated his actions of the week before, and Timmy was returned home. Later, one of the other children being molested by Mr. Thompson reported the abuse, and an investigation was begun.

When the investigation finally got to Timmy and the abuse was discovered, Timmy's parents were devastated. They had missed his signals. After several months of counseling, Timmy disclosed some of his feelings. He had communicated to his parents that he did not want to go with Mr. Thompson, but because his father made him go the second time, Timmy thought his parents knew what was happening to him and that it was OK with them.

Changes in School Performance

A child may exhibit signs of being an underachiever by displaying poor concentration or by daydreaming. A child could be labelled "learning disabled," but may, in reality, be under the chronic stress of an abusive situation. The classic profile of the withdrawn child with a low self-image is not always an indicator, however. The image of the overachieving "perfect" child who is overly compliant in trying to please adults can be another face that hides the secret of abuse.

Self-Injury/Graphic Play

Sometimes a child acts out the stress of the abuse by self-injurious behaviors such as biting themselves or others, cutting themselves, or by destructive, continuous masturbation. Perhaps a child will reveal the trauma of abuse by drawing pictures of adults' or children's genitals, especially with details like pubic hair.

Feeling "Bad"

A child betrayed by a trusted person has received the message that he or she is a "bad" child. Such children often feel tremendous guilt and shame in conflict with any positive feelings they may have for the offender. In order to shroud the secret, this conflict must be hidden as well. This may make it necessary for the child to move from the point of always "pretending" everything is OK to the point of becoming a skillful liar. Reality can evolve from black and white to indistinct shades of gray.

Loss of Personal Identity

Sexual abuse is a violation of personal boundaries and confuses the child about his identity and his body. Some children may avoid all physical contact with others and refuse to be held, hugged, or cuddled. Others may appear listless, detached, or isolated. The child can come to think that he or she is an "extension" of the offender. Feeling somehow responsible to meet the needs of the offender, the child often complies with the abuse at the expense of personal boundaries and losing his or her identity as an individual.

Precocious Sexuality

Sometimes a young child will have been taught by being sexually exploited that "favors" can be earned through sexual behavior. When Tom and Edna Smith went to visit Edna's sister, one of the sister's day-care children crawled up onto the couch where Tom was sitting. As the little girl reached over nonchalantly and unzipped Tom's pants, Tom was horrified, and he and Edna left the home immediately. Unfortunately, his surprise and disgust did not motivate him to pursue the incident further. Ten years later, when that little girl was 14 and pregnant, the crisis pregnancy center discovered that she had been sexually abused by her stepfather for several years as a child and had learned that sex was the way to get love and attention.

Signals of Abuse in Adolescence

Physical Signals

The transition from prepubescence to adolescence adds new dimensions to the symptoms already described. Some of the same physical signs might be present, with the addition of pregnancy and/or psychosomatic complaints such as chronic abdominal pain, gastric distress, or headaches. Having bowel movements in underwear and bed-wetting could continue to be a signal. One woman reported wetting the bed until she was 20 years old, but no one had ever thought to ask why.

Eating Disorders

Sometimes anorexia, bulimia, or other eating disorders can be a response to abuse. Anorectic individuals may literally starve themselves by a regimented system of not eating. The person with bulimic behavior will compulsively overeat in binges and then attempt to get rid of the extra calories by forced vomiting or purging their system with excessive laxatives. Eating disorders or overeating may be the only outlet for stress in an abusive family system where rigidity and emotional suppression are modeled. Abuse can distort the body image of the individual. Eating disorders can be a desperate attempt to correct the body image, to maintain some kind of control when life seems out of control, to punish oneself for being bad or to deal with the pain of suppressed feelings.

Withdrawal

Young children with poor concentration may become withdrawn and emotionally constricted adolescents. They may exhibit a marked lack of insight due to the developmental deficit created by the abusive relationship. This inability to interact emotionally with others may severely impair the abused adolescent in relationships. One 16-year-old incest victim, even though placed in a loving and secure foster home, was so withdrawn that she did not speak for three months. At night, she would wedge her bedroom dresser against the door to prevent intrusion. She would place coat hangers on the doorknobs in the hallway leading to her room so they would make noise signalling anyone's approach. Withdrawal, fear, and distrust are inevitable responses to abuse.

Isolation

The child who avoided all touch may become the isolated and withdrawn teen who concludes, "I don't need *anybody*!" Such withdrawal may lead to a pattern of setting others up to reject them; this reinforces the isolation but provides a protection against intimacy.

Dependency

Conversely, the overly compliant child may become the very dependent adolescent who is unable to withstand any type of rejection, and will follow peers at any cost. Because of personal boundaries being violated or blurred, survival for this adolescent may come in the form of being sexually used. The young child who earned favors for being sexually abused may become a manipulative, seductive, sexually active adolescent who views him or herself, as well as others, as sex objects.

Self-abuse

The self-abusive behavior of the young child can intensify during the teen years. Cutting the flesh, slitting wrists, burning the body with cigarettes, especially in the breast or genital areas, can be desperate signals of abuse. One adolescent melted the skin on her forearms with a hot iron in an effort to signal her distress. Destructive and self-abusive masturbation can continue from childhood into adolescence and can become an obsessive preoccupation. Tattoos can occasionally be a form of self-injurious behavior. Suicidal thoughts and suicide attempts are frequently signs of abuse.

Running Away

Running away can be a "red flag" signal that an adolescent may be an abuse victim. When running away from home is not possible, other creative "running" can be evidenced—"running away" into a room, or "running away" into fantasy as a place to escape reality and pain.

Distrust

The betrayal of trust and fear of exposure that was planted in the young child can grow into compulsive lying and distrustfulness of others, especially distrust of authority figures. The messages of shame and guilt projected onto the child in early years by significant people in the child's life can now be internally generated by the teen. Low self-image and feelings of inherent worthlessness are unavoidable results of continual and hidden abuse.

Role Reversal

Sometimes a prepubescent child will exhibit a pseudo-maturity and seem capable of handling adult responsibilities, especially in areas of home management and child care. This may be a "mask" of role reversal, where the child has taken on the parent's role as care-giver in the home. In incest cases, the role reversal often extends into the sexual relationship, where the wife's sexual responsibilities are required of the daughter, or the husband's emotional care for his wife is lacking and the mother turns to the son.

Acting Out

The emotions repressed in the young child can present themselves overtly in adolescence. Intensely painful emotions are revealed in "acting out." Acting out can appear as rebellion against authority figures: arson, violence, stealing, cruelty to animals, promiscuity, having intentional "accidents," chemical use/abuse, physical or sexual abuse of self or others, vandalism, incorrigibility, depression, or eating disorders, as well as other displays of negative behavior.

Sexual Identity Confusion

Another symptom of sexual abuse that surfaces in adolescence arises in the area of sexual identity. As the abuse violates a child's personal boundaries and brings confusion about individual identity, so also comes confusion about sexual identity. Both same-sex and opposite-sex abuse may plunge victims into confusion over their own sexuality. Dysfunctional family systems and destructive sexual relationships communicate negative messages that contribute to painful confusion in the area of sexuality. It is common for abused children and adolescents to despise their gender or specific parts of their body due to degrading messages, which, transmitted through the abusive relationship, have been translated into a distorted body image.

Impact of Abuse in Adult Life

Adult manifestations of abuse can be a sophistication or "cementing in" of any of the effects already mentioned. As defense mechanisms take up residence in the adult victim who has not worked through the recovery process, the adult will most likely experience dysfunctional relationships—perfectionism, passive dependencies or over-control—and feel defeated in many areas of life. Commonly, adult victims will see no connection between their present situations and their past history of abuse. One way they block the pain of the past is through denial or minimizing the effects: "That happened so long ago. It has no effect on me now. It really wasn't a big deal. I shouldn't let it bother me anymore." Such statements indicate that the person is fighting to deny that the abuse was either painful or significant in their life.

A common adult response to abuse is perfectionism and "over-proving" themselves. This can be motivated by believing messages that said: *You never measure up. You're defective. You're unlovable/unwanted. Your feelings are not important. You are bad for having needs.* Shame is emotionally crippling and convinces people that they are bad, worthless, and of no value. Shame is the basis for many "cover-up" kinds of behavior, trying through performance to earn approval from God and others. An attitude of contempt for and shaming of others may be another mask used to hide the shame of abuse. Always having to be right is another way to combat the shaming messages from the abuse; rage, or being forceful and angry, can also be a cover to hide shame and to keep others at a distance to avoid intimacy.

The adult victim may discover ways to mask or alter these shame messages, at least temporarily. Chemical abuse, eating disorders, promiscuity, or workaholism can be behavioral responses to the shame of abuse, as can compulsive overspending, compulsive overeating, or other compulsive behaviors.

Acting out in the adult can come through suicide attempts, hospitalizations (often for chronic depression) or allowing "injuries" to happen. The acting out of learned behavior through promiscuity or prostitution bears the negative fruit of Prov. 22:6: "Train up a child in the way he should go, and when he is old, he will not depart from it." Unless there is intervention, many children "trained up" by sexually abusive relationships will not "depart from" those kinds of relationships when they are adults.

Interpersonal relationships are greatly affected by an abusive history. One dysfunctional way an adult might try to have relationships is in care-taking and being overresponsible for everyone and everything that happens. Such behavior patterns may outwardly seem to be positive traits, but they result in a perpetuation of dysfunctional relationships and an inability to relate in a positive, healthy manner.

The Performance Syndrome

Although adult victims may isolate and insulate themselves from others, sexually abused individuals may not always experience social ineptitude. They may appear to be "together" and "on top of things," but this is only one face of living two lives. Such a person is aware of looking OK but constantly fears the exposure or revealing of the bad person within.

One 47-year-old woman was a "perfect," very spiritual pastor's wife. She would constantly give of herself to others, listen to and care about everyone's problems. In addition, she was the perfect example of submission to the congregation and was looked up to as a role model of the Christian life. What she never shared with anyone was her chronic depression, for which there was "no reason," and her paralyzing fear of inadequacy as a wife and mother.

When she finally shared with someone about a few incidents of sexual contact between her father and her, she concluded by saying that she loved her father and had forgiven him and that there were now no effects of abuse in her life. She followed some strong urging to see a counselor, and was able to identify some of the negative and shaming messages that she had been carrying with her since childhood. She was able to see how that shame and guilt and fear of being found out had motivated her to "perform" and to look perfect *at all times.* She began to see how her depression had been a signal that she was being crushed under the load of her past, and she was able to break through the denial and minimizing to begin the recovery process.

Passive Dependence

Another unhealthy way of relating is in passive dependencies. A person may experience life as a "doormat," feeling helpless and having no control over life. Such people may give up many areas of personal responsibility and want others to take care of them. This disguise for protection (not consciously perceived by the individual) communicates to others, "I am helpless; I am weak; I can't make it without you because I'm not OK in myself." Helplessness can be a very powerful way to control others and absolve oneself of personal accountability. Such people may feel it is safer to let others take most of life's risks for them, and they often live their lives vicariously through others.[1] Dependence proves destructive to forming healthy relationships because those who try to get close tend to feel "used" and "drained dry" by the dependent person.

A Need to Control

Another unsatisfying relationship pattern revolves around a need to control. A person might find that the only way to feel

---

[1]Connie Stevens and Anna Gates, *Freed!*, 10. Available at Canyon House #10, Canyon Park NSR, Boulder, CO, 80302. The cost is $5.00. *Freed!* does not deal with sexual abuse specifically but with general principles in relationships within the context of Christian faith.

secure is to be in control at all times. A situation that places a person at risk of failure or vulnerability can trigger an intense fear of not being in control.

Perhaps this kind of control will emerge in a person who is "always right" or someone who is over-controlling in his parenting. A contemptuous attitude toward others can be a way of being in control, as can careful attention to appearing "all together" in front of others. The need to look good in front of others may influence a person to choose relationships with people who will make them look good. This pattern is usually subconscious, and such people may not be aware of the danger until they are married to an alcoholic, deeply entangled with a mentally ill person, chief "hand-holder" of self-determined failures, or involved with someone else with a problem.[2]

Sexual Dysfunction

Adult attitudes about sexuality resulting from abuse are varied and painful. An individual may feel that sex is dirty, immoral, or bad, and will, therefore, be unable to accept or experience any sexual pleasure within a marriage relationship. A woman may feel intensely shameful if she experienced any pleasure during her abuse and may now try to shut down those feelings and only try to comply with her husband to meet his needs. Sometimes wives cannot "unfreeze" themselves due to a behavior pattern of dissociation, a numbing of themselves physically and emotionally during the sexual acts of the abuse. Sometimes it is difficult for a woman to relinquish control and respond sexually to her husband because she was stimulated against her will in the past. She may also fear being forced to be hurt in some way, or fear being used.

A common and extremely painful occurrence is the suffering of "flashbacks"—vivid mental images of past events—triggered by current circumstances. These flashbacks are very distressing to the abused person because the triggering event activates painful memories that wash over the individual with a wave of intensity. It is also distressing to the spouse or whoever triggered the flashback, as they are likely to receive a negative response

---

[2]Ibid.

that seems inappropriate to the situation.

One woman found herself reacting with revulsion to her husband when he would shower prior to approaching her sexually. It only happened intermittently, however, and caused her intense shame and guilt for having such a hostile response to her husband at these times, especially since he did not deserve it and it confused and hurt him deeply. In counseling, it was discovered that the smell of a certain brand of soap triggered the memory of her abusive father, who always showered with that soap before he was sexual with her.

Sometimes abuse victims alternate between two extremes in sexual behavior: complete aversion to sex or compulsive sexual activity. Single women who would like a family but have an aversion to sex may feel doubly frustrated by not fitting into a "couples" society and by being unable to overcome fear, repulsion and distrust of men.

Compulsive sexual behavior has very little to do with enjoying or desiring sex, but can instead be an attempt to overcome painful isolation and/or seek affection. Fearing intimacy and lacking trust in men, however, a woman may be unable to form a stable relationship. Casual sexual encounters can seem more "safe," because the more intimate a relationship becomes, the more frightening it is.

As in adolescence, sexual identity and sexual orientation can be an area of confusion and pain for the adult victim. A woman may feel she has sexual "power" over men in her body, but she may view it as destructive. Many have seen how sexual feelings have taken control of others and this feeling can be frightening.

A negative and distorted body image may convince victims that they are ugly, and an abused person may deliberately try to appear ugly or unattractive. One woman, for example, wore thick glasses, feeling safer to be behind her glasses than to be noticed by men. Another woman, 5 feet tall, gained until she weighed 235 pounds, guaranteeing that she would not be abused again because she was so overweight and unattractive.

Abused women can also have a real mistrust of women as well, due to much unresolved bitterness toward a mother who did not protect them, or toward a mother or mother-figure who sexually abused them.

A man who has been sexually abused by his mother is perhaps the most silent of all victims. An incestuous father can "force" his victim, but an incestuous mother must seduce her son in order to maintain sexual arousal and/or an erection. The pseudo-tenderness makes it difficult for the male victim to recognize his emotional pain and unresolved inner conflicts. Because there seems to be no element of force, the male victim almost invariably comes away with guilt feelings. Most commonly, he will feel like an accomplice rather than a victim. The frequency of mother/son incest involving actual sexual intercourse is less common than the seductive fondling of a son by a mother. Although this may seem less overt, it is equally destructive to the male victim and contributes to insecurity, extreme self-consciousness, and discomfort around women. Without intervention, this male victim may become an adult who acts out his inner anguish by beating his wife, abusing his daughter, or raping women.

Male victims of father-son incest can feel deep depressive symptoms of self-loathing, sexual identity problems, and difficulty in relationships with both men and women. If the male victim hates his father, who is his role model, he hates a large part of himself. This male victim experiences a loss of masculine identity and dignity.[3] He lives with painfully damaged emotions, but may feel unable to express his need for help because pain is not consistent with a "macho" male image.

These effects of sexual abuse do not represent a total scenario but rather a composite of some of the more common results of abuse. Such abuse can influence the whole person physically, emotionally, behaviorally, psychologically, and spiritually. The effects, though predictable, cannot be stereotyped; the scars of sexual abuse are as varied as the faces who hide them. But abuse impacts a person's whole life, from childhood through adolescence to adulthood.

---

[3]Susan Forward and Craig Buck, *Betrayal Of Innocence: Incest and Its Devastation* (Los Angeles: Jeremy P. Tarcher, Inc.).

◊ **4** ◊

Spiritual Damage

Elizabeth was brought up in a Christian home; all the family members were professing Christians who attended church whenever the doors were open. She made a decision for Christ at an early age and experienced a normal, uneventful childhood until the abuse began. Elizabeth's Uncle Phil, himself a professing Christian, had always been affectionate with her. But when she was 10 years old, he started french kissing her and fondling her. He told her not to tell anyone—it would be just their "little secret." He said if she did tell, Aunt Mary would divorce him and her parents would be very upset with her.

Elizabeth had been carefully taught that a good Christian girl must obey her elders, and so she did. Once, early in the abuse relationship, Elizabeth tried to tell her mom that her uncle was putting his hand down inside her blouse. Her mom became angry with her for showing her mother what he was doing and said, "Oh, his hand must have slipped. He would never do anything wrong." Elizabeth never talked to her mom about it again, and the abuse continued.

Elizabeth's uncle used his Christian faith as a means to abuse her. He lived out-of-state but made frequent visits to Elizabeth's family. During his visits, at mealtimes, he always wanted Elizabeth to sit next to him. While he was praying, he would be touching her under the table. Sometimes at night, he would come into her bedroom, telling her, "Say your prayers like a good girl," then would fondle her after she prayed. Elizabeth was very confused about God. Is this what He wanted for her? She prayed, "God, stop Uncle Phil!" But the abuse went on.

Her uncle became more forceful in his expectations of her. He started having sexual intercourse with her and had her perform oral sex on him. Her guilt, shame, and confusion mounted. Didn't God care about her? Was He powerless? Why didn't God answer her prayers? Elizabeth didn't understand how Uncle Phil could be a Christian and do these things to her. She became very angry with God and didn't want to go to church. When she did go, she felt guilty and dirty and was sure that others could see right through her and know her terrible secret.

Elizabeth worried about her younger sisters; she felt that if she did not let her uncle abuse her, he might start to abuse her sisters. So she decided to sacrifice herself in order to protect her sisters from harm.

After the abuse had gone on for seven years, Elizabeth could no longer remain silent. She told a Sunday school teacher about the abuse. The secret was out. What would happen now? Would all those bad things happen that he had threatened? The police were called in; Uncle Phil was taken to jail and had to have some brief counseling sessions. That was all. Aunt Mary did not divorce him.

Elizabeth's parents reacted to the abuse situation by telling her it was "all over now." She was to "forgive and forget," to "put it behind her." Rage about this injustice seethed within her. Why hadn't her Christian parents protected her from him in the first place? She had never been told anything like this could happen. Why hadn't they listened to her when she tried to tell them about the abuse? Why couldn't they understand how much pain she was going through now that her horrible shame was exposed? Why wouldn't they support her by at least trying to understand the intensity of the pain she had endured for so long?

New information came to light when it was discovered that Uncle Phil had also been abusing two of Elizabeth's sisters. He had told her sisters that because Elizabeth was cooperating, they should, too. Elizabeth's personal pain and shame increased intensely; now she felt responsible for what had happened to her sisters.

At this point, Elizabeth was not only angry with the powerless, absent, unfair God she perceived, but with her parents, her uncle, and most of all, herself. She became rebellious, and she started drinking and using drugs to numb her pain. Confused about her sexuality, she became sexually active with both boys and girls. Her anger at God came out sideways in many violations of His moral laws as she unconsciously tried to "get even" with Him for her uncle's violations of her. Her God had become a cosmic "kill-joy," an unpleasable taskmaster, a punitive parent/judge who delivered punishment for every wrong thought, feeling and action. She wanted to die, and after an attempted suicide, she ended up confined in a psychiatric ward for a week trying to straighten herself out.

Not long after being released from the hospital, Elizabeth met a Christian young woman who showed her love, care, and acceptance. This was the first person who had ever really loved her just for herself. Elizabeth's inner pain and extreme neediness motivated her to become unhealthily dependent on her new friend, and within months, this woman had become her lover. She knew she was making wrong choices, but her dependency on other people was in control. She was inwardly split between the intellectual knowledge that homosexual activity was sinful and the emotional intensity of fearing abandonment, wrestling with feelings of having no other "source" to meet her needs for security and worth.

Elizabeth began attending a Christian college, hoping that being there would help her be a "better" Christian and quiet the dark memories of her past. Her past did not go away, however, nor did the guilt of her same-sex relationship. She felt like a hypocrite. The required Bible classes only made her feel more guilty. Her inner conflicts and guilt mounted to an almost unbearable point, and she finally came to a crossroads experience in her life.

She felt there was nowhere else to go and nothing more to lose, so she decided to try to discover what God was really like. She wondered if He could, or would, help her. Through attending a Christian sexual abuse support group in conjunction with individual counseling, she was able to work through enough of the pain to begin to see God as He really is. Her image of the unfair-taskmaster God softened in the face of His empathy, compassion, and unconditional acceptance of her. She began to experience some of His love, forgiveness and presence in her daily life. It will take years before she will be able to resolve all the problems resulting from her abuse, and from the denial and rejection of her parents. She is, however, beginning to experience freedom from the heavy burden she has carried for so many years.

The emotional and spiritual damage in Elizabeth's life was devastating, crippling—it almost caused her to take her life. Her questions were intense and valid, and needing answers. How could she trust the God of her uncle who prayed as he abused her? How could she trust the God of her parents who didn't protect her, and then, when the abuse was revealed, didn't understand or support her? How could an all-loving God allow a little girl to suffer abuse for seven years?

Spiritual Effects of Violation

The sexual violation of a child has many spiritual effects. A distorted image of God, coupled with a distorted image of self, creates multiple barriers to experiencing God's presence in the healing process or His love in other facets of life.

A distorted image of self, feelings of being worthless, rejected, insignificant, or abandoned can either compound or result from the spiritual damage wrought by abuse. Elizabeth's history illustrates many of these areas of spiritual damage.

Distorted Images of God

Each child comes into the world equipped with an unclear perception of God. Because at the Fall, God suddenly looked "different" to Adam and Eve; they became afraid and hid. That fallen nature and distorted image of God is now an integral part of each person's spiritual being. If a child grows up without personally knowing and experiencing Christ, that child will come to acknowledge those distortions about God as truth, rather than as the result of fallen humanity. Distortions about God take many forms: God is dead or nonexistent, He is impotent, He is an impossible taskmaster, a celestial "kill-joy," or perhaps a "Santa Claus" in the sky keeping track of whether we're naughty or nice.[1] Viewed through Elizabeth's eyes, it is understandable that her "God" was a punitive parent and judge

---

[1]Dr. David Seamands, "Healing Distorted Concepts of God" (Minneapolis, Minn.: National Counseling Conference, Crystal Free Evangelical Church, May 14–16, 1986).

whose only involvement in her life was to punish her.

Because a child cannot automatically correct such false assumptions, God designed a plan to assist each individual in coming to know Him as He really is. One of the primary means through which a child experiences the reality of God is through his or her parents. God instituted parenting as a preliminary introduction to His grace. He began with Adam and Eve, who surely instructed their children about relating to God through the sacrificial system in Gen. 4:3–4, and He even "parented" Christ through Mary and Joseph. Parents were to be a representation of God's agape love—a balance of love and limits, of affection and discipline.[2]

When parents abuse or neglect their children, those intended "agents" of God's grace not only reinforce the child's fallen perception of God, but actually become tools of destruction. Sometimes children are even abused in God's name, being told it is God's will for them to submit to the abuse in order to "be obedient to their parents."

One woman recalls early memories of her father exposing his genitals to her and forcing her to touch him. As she got older, he would systematically abuse both the male and female children, and then read verses from the Bible about honoring your father and "loving" one another. She viewed God as a punitive, inconsistent God who always demanded more from her than she was able to give, and who punished her for not measuring up. Similarly, Elizabeth's uncle, an elder in her church, used religious practices such as prayer as an opportunity to abuse and confuse Elizabeth's view of God.

In cases where children are abused by nonfamily members, there may still be compounded spiritual damage if the child fears he or she will not be believed, will be punished, or feels unable to tell and thus unprotected. God is sometimes viewed as inept, undiscerning, or powerless. A 25-year-old woman reported feeling very afraid to tell her parents about being abused as a child of 7 by a teenage neighbor boy. As a child, she was convinced they would blame her for causing trouble. Only "happy Christian feelings" were allowed in her home; other feelings were sinful and not allowed. In her late 20's, she sought

---

[2]Ibid.

professional counseling for depression.

As she slowly unraveled her thoughts and feelings, she began to realize the effects of the shame, anger, fear and pain she had buried inside, not only from the abuse, but from the inability to get support from her parents. She became aware, for the first time, that deep inside she had come to this conclusion: Only a "jerk" would allow a little kid to *be* hurt and then be mad at them for *feeling* hurt. Based on the role-modeling of her parents and their denial of feelings, she had long ago decided that God must be a "jerk" too, someone who was detached and inept. Her concept of God had effectively isolated her from being able to relate to Him on a personal level, even though she was actively involved in ministry.

Distorted Images of Self

Our concept of God is a composite of theology (what we believe about God and what we believe God thinks about us) and our experiences in interpersonal relationships (what we believe about ourselves and what we believe others think of us). Thus our concept of God is the sum total of our life experience.[3]

Elizabeth learned many things about God at church that were not reflected in her everyday life experience. As the abuse continued, she felt increasingly negative about herself and felt somehow responsible for causing the abuse. She became angry with God for not protecting her from the abuse. Her self-hate and her hate for God became one.

Elizabeth's experience is an example of how incredibly difficult it is for victims of sexual abuse to respond positively or freely to God's grace. More often than not, God is perceived as being absent when needed instead of present and available; of being unjust and unfair instead of being holy and just; of being a punitive parent/judge who, at the slightest failure, hands out condemnation, rather than a God of unconditional grace.[4]

One young woman told of trying to please God by attempting to increase her own suffering during the years of her abuse. She believed, as she had been taught, that "suffering makes Jesus like you better and means He loves you more." At age 10, she

---

[3]Ibid.
[4]Ibid.

knelt for five hours on broken pieces of hard macaroni—the closest thing to broken glass that she could think of—and begged God not to love her anymore. Who would not experience fear, bitterness, or anger toward such a God?

Just as emotional damage results from the disruption of interpersonal relationships between the child and significant others, so spiritual damage comes from a disrupted interpersonal relationship with God. Even a sincere adult believer can harbor such a warped inner childhood image of God as to be unable to *feel* personally intimate with or unconditionally accepted by Him. The matter of sincerity worsens the problem because often the victimized person studies Scripture and prays steadfastly, knowing intellectual truth but not experiencing a real sense of relationship with God. This person realizes something is wrong but, not understanding the effects of the spiritual damage of abuse, blames him/herself for failing once again to please God.

"What did I do so wrong that God let this happen to me?" wept Janice in one of her first counseling sessions. "I try so hard to make up for being a bad little girl, and I really do want to be a good Christian. But, somehow, I always end up letting God down." Janice interpreted her emotional struggles as spiritual problems, without realizing that her view of God from her childhood was so distorted that an adult relationship with Him proved very difficult.

Another area of spiritual damage surfaces when the victims become "dependent" on God so that He can "use" them. Relinquishing control of their life to God is fearful for victims, because they have learned that dependent vulnerability is the essence of victimization. A common and necessary problem for most victims to work through is the question, "Where was God during the time the abuse was happening, and what part does He play in the healing process?" After having been sexually "used" by someone older and more powerful, one woman reacted with rage to the idea of going through the painful healing process in order to then be "used" by God. Thus the "good news" can become the "bad news" to someone with a distorted image of God and His purposes.

One adolescent came to grips with this issue by defining victimization as "when you have no choice" and dependence on God as "when you can ask for help." For her, the difference between victimization and dependence on God was the issue of choice. A person who is dependent on God has the freedom to choose that dependency, rather than experience again the helplessness of victimization in which there are no choices.

Helping the Victim

Many victims feel the way Elizabeth did, having tremendous anger toward God, their parents and other Christians who did not understand the deep pain the abuse victim has endured. Many pastors and other Christians are personally uncomfortable or unfamiliar with such intense pain. Wanting to "rescue" the victim as well as to avoid experiencing their own pain through personal involvement, they may tend to give "formulas" or "pat answer" solutions: "Just trust in Jesus and everything will be OK."

Initially, however, such superficial advice only increases the pain and confusion victims experience. It implies that they don't have enough faith, that they should be "OK" by now, or that they are not pleasing to God in some way because they aren't yet healed. Sometimes when an advisor admonishes "Just give it to the Lord," he may really mean, "Don't give it to me! I don't want to be involved." Christ is the Healer; He wants to heal the damage that has been done, but restoration often involves a process that takes years. There is no "quick fix" to the pain of sexual abuse.

Without first repairing the interpersonal relationship with God (the reconciliation spoken of in 2 Cor. 5:18–21), the abuse victim has no "source" with which to establish any lasting victory over the results of damage in his or her life, nor sustenance for the journey to wholeness. Many times the relationship with God must be entirely role-modeled again within a trusting and caring counseling relationship as the victim learns how to have a healthy relationship with another person as a pattern for developing a healthy relationship with the person of Christ.

Dealing with spiritual damage is a significant part of the recovery process. Practical helps in facilitating that process are presented in Chapter 10: Step Two.

Section Two

Understanding the Abusive Family

◊ **5** ◊

Incest: The Ultimate Betrayal

By God's design, the primary channel for learning one's identity, for having needs met, for understanding who God is, and for developing relationships is the family system. John Bettler, writing in the *Institute of Biblical Counseling Perspective*, states that "man as the image of God exists in two parts, male and female."[1] Both male and female components, in the role of mother and father in a family system, directly affect our composite image of God, of self, and of interpersonal relationships.

In families where one or both parents represent distortions of God within that family system, relationships will be skewed and pain will result. First Cor. 12:26 illustrates how every part of the Body (or a family) suffers when one part suffers. This is true both in families where incest is occurring or where abuse is occurring by a perpetrator outside the family, but the family is unaware of it.

Scripture speaks to incestuous family systems with the principle found in Gal. 5:9: "A little leaven leavens the whole lump." Families involved in incest have several common denominators, and each individual is impacted by the "leaven" in that system. Once the family system is understood, intervention then becomes possible. Restoration will only be complete as each individual takes responsibility before God and other family members to correct the dysfunctions.

The Incestuous Family

Incest happens in families of all types, regardless of economic, educational, social, cultural, or religious backgrounds.

---

[1] John F. Bettler, "Understanding Sexual Identity," vol. 1, no. 1, *Insitute of Biblical Counseling Perspective* (A publication of the Institute of Biblical Counseling, Winona Lake, Indiana, 1985), 50.

Because of the almost universal taboo against incest, many people have believed the myth that incest does not happen within Christian families and, therefore, is not a subject the church needs to address.

Incest *must* be addressed by the church, however; many offenders have a Christian background and may even use the church as a guise for their abuse. In fact, many offenders are leaders in their community or church—as was the case for some of the women mentioned in Section One. Elizabeth's uncle, for example, was an elder in an evangelical church and worked with children in the Sunday school department. Julie's father was also a respected church leader. As difficult as it might be to admit, the church community has a need to acknowledge that sexual abuse is a possibility in any congregation. In fairness to the children God has created, we must face the reality that the possibility of incest exists within Christian families. The church needs to have an open and sensitive spirit to be able to detect the symptoms of incestuous families so that those family members will be able to get the help they need.

Incest: Looking Beneath the Mask

The church never saw beneath the mask of the Taylor family. The family attended church faithfully and centered its entertainment around church activities.

Though a petite and fragile-looking woman, Mrs. Taylor seemed to have endless talents for giving and serving. Immaculate about her appearance, she kept the house in near perfect order and had three lovely children—a daughter and two sons. Her frequent illnesses caused much concern to those who knew her, but she remained faithful to her responsibilities as Sunday school superintendent, Christian Ed director, and missions committee chairwoman. She projected the image of the perfect wife and mother.

Mr. Taylor was the choir director and the adult Sunday school pastor-teacher. He often taught about the sins of society and encouraged those in his class to abstain from worldly pursuits such as drinking, dancing, and movies. As a result of his strong discipline in his household, his children were well behaved and obedient.

Because of her fragile health, Mrs. Taylor demanded much care from their daughter Melanie. Melanie thus fulfilled the role of "Mom's little helper" and learned very young that she would get the "cold shoulder" silent treatment from Mom if she wasn't helpful enough cleaning the house or caring for her little brothers. Even though Melanie's mother would express physical affection, somehow Melanie never felt that she pleased her mother unless she did a perfect job with her home chores.

Melanie tried not to do anything to make her father angry. She knew from the violent spankings her brothers received that she must be careful never to upset him. Questioning her father was not allowed because he was her authority, and saying no was considered to be rebellious. Melanie sensed a tension between her parents—in reality, a lack of intimacy—and felt it to be her responsibility to make sure she did not upset them. At church, she learned that anger was a sin and that to resolve conflict in a relationship, she needed to "fix" herself because she was the problem for having the anger.

When Melanie was 7, her father phoned from work one afternoon and said he would be coming home to see if she had been obedient in doing her chores. She quickly finished cleaning the kitchen for his approval. When he walked in, he sent her brothers out to play, took her into the bedroom, put a knife in the lock on the door so no one could come in, fondled her and digitally penetrated her while he masturbated. From then on, he routinely came home in the afternoon to abuse her while her mother was at work. He attempted intercourse on occasion but was unable to penetrate her small body. He would often want to take her for a ride in the car, and he would fondle her and masturbate while driving. Her father always told her, "Don't tell your mother; it will kill her. If she finds out, she'll die, and it will be your fault."

The intensity of the shame, fear, and rage was "stuffed" deep inside Melanie's soul as the abuse continued for years. When she was 13, three of her aunts approached her, concerned that her father might attempt to "touch her wrong." Then Melanie learned that her father had been having sexual relationships with these aunts, her mother's sisters, and that they had come to warn her. She broke down and cried, telling them it was already too late.

Her aunts reported the abuse to the authorities, and Melanie's father was picked up by the police. However, a consuming fear remained. Due to her mother's "fragile health," everyone feared exposing the secret. Mrs. Taylor was escorted to her doctor's office, where her sisters told her about the sexual abuse. Melanie, sitting outside the room, could hear her mother screaming and was terrified that the information might, in fact, kill her. When her aunts came out of the doctor's office, they told Melanie that her dad was now in prison and that she didn't have to be afraid to go home. Alone with her mother in the car on the way home, Melanie's mother looked intently at her 13-year-old daughter and asked, "How could you do this to me? You took my husband away. . . ."

How could the church have been an instrument of healing for the Taylor family? What could have been done after the incest was reported? In Melanie's case, the church failed her entirely. No one ever mentioned the incident again. No one encouraged her to seek counseling or even recognized that she was paralyzed with pain. No one visited her father in prison or helped Mrs. Taylor to see the role she played in the incest. Melanie grew up in a family that went on as if "nothing had happened" and ignored her, except for occasionally reminding her that she had ruined the family.

Melanie later married, endured an abusive relationship with her husband for 12 years, went through the shame and stigma of divorce, and remarried only to become victimized again. At 45, on the brink of an emotional collapse, she finally sought counseling and began to discover the truth about incest, about who she was and about who God is. She agreed to describe her trauma in this book so that others would be encouraged to look beneath the mask to see that incest does exist in their churches.

In order to be equipped to intervene in the incestuous family, pastors, counselors, and other helpers will need to be aware first that incest is a possibility in *their* church. In addition to this awareness, however, there is also a need for specific knowledge about incest and about effective ways to help those who are currently being abused and those who were abused in the past, as well as their family members.

◊ **6** ◊

Intervention in Incest

Studies show that most often incest develops in multi-problem families. Certain aspects of dysfunctional families emerge as trouble spots, problem areas that create an environment which can foster abuse. Difficulties may be discovered in general areas such as:

1. Self-worth—the feelings and ideas family members have about themselves;
2. Communication—the ways people attempt to have meaningful interaction;
3. The family system—the rules that govern how family members feel and act;
4. The link to society—how family members relate to each other and to institutions outside the family.[1]

Specific problem areas common to incest families are presented below. To assist the pastor or counselor in guiding families through the recovery process, treatment goals and practical tools of intervention follow the discussion of each problem area. Family counseling is the treatment of choice in most incest cases, but family counseling should not begin until counseling relationships have been established with individual family members. A family assessment should be conducted to identify the strengths and weaknesses of that family's system. Assessing the following problem areas will help the counselor determine the degree and type of family pathology.

---

[1]Virginia Satir, *Peoplemaking* (Palo Alto, Calif.: Science and Behavior Books, 1972).

Shame

Shame is like cancer of the spirit, an inherent feeling of defectiveness, of "not measuring up" as a person. Understanding shame is foundational for understanding incest. In Melanie's case, her family's entire system was rooted in shame prior to the incest, with the incest being one outgrowth of that shame. The degree to which people are convinced that they are loved unconditionally; that they are valuable, gifted and special; and that they are not alone to face life's struggles is the same degree to which they will be able to love, serve and build others up. The degree to which individuals are *not* convinced of these things is the same degree to which they will function out of emptiness and shame.[2]

The curse of shame, which passes from one generation to the next, perpetuating all forms of abuse, began in the garden with Adam and Eve. The fact that they lost their "life" (their source of unconditional love, their source of value and belonging) establishes the defectiveness of human beings. The impossibility of regaining "life" or earning God's approval through personal performance leaves each individual unable to correct this defectiveness.[3] Many sources of "life" can be sought to correct this inherent defectiveness, but only the free gift of grace through Jesus Christ can replace spiritual death with life and enable us to be convinced of His love and our value.[4]

Members of incest families are like empty circles:

---

[2]Jeff VanVonderen, *Good News for the Chemically Dependent* (Nashville, Tenn.: Thomas Nelson Publishers, 1985), 78–80.
[3]Ibid., 83.
[4]Ibid., 87.

The inner circle represents the void that yearns for love, acceptance, value, meaning, purpose in life—indeed, life itself. This kind of inner life cannot be earned, bought or discovered.[5] Spiritual life can only be *received* as a gift because of *Christ's* "performance"—His love flowing to us out of His fullness, rather than coming to us based on *our* "performance," our good works.

The outer circle in this diagram represents the behaviors people use to cover their emptiness so others cannot see their inner defectiveness. These behaviors may be positive or negative, depending on the "others" that the person is trying to please. If any behavior is motivated by an inner sense of not measuring up, whether that behavior looks positive or negative on the outside, it acts as a barrier to healthy relationships and predisposes the person to look for ways to fill the void within.

In the Taylor family, Mr. Taylor's emptiness was not filled from the fullness of Christ. Rather, he masked his emptiness by being choir director and pastor-teacher to the adult Sunday school class. In order to be accepted in his church, he believed he had to be active and successful in ministry. He required his daughter to memorize certain sounds so that, at age 7, she would appear to be speaking in tongues. He told her it didn't look good for Daddy to have a disobedient daughter who wasn't "filled with the Spirit." In order to be acceptable as a man, he had to be the head of his household by keeping his children in subjection. He believed that in order to have God's approval, he had to follow a rigid discipline of daily devotions and Bible study. When he was not able to keep to this goal, however, he felt his lack of discipline (performance, in his case) proved he was a failure.

Underneath all of his "Christian behavior" was the gnawing emptiness that comes from feeling unloved, worthless, and alone. He was raw and needy on the inside—a shamed and shaming father. Instead of looking to the available sufficiency of Christ for his source of life, he turned to his wife. When his wife proved too preoccupied to meet his needs, he demanded that those needs for value, nurture, and self-importance be met by his daughter.

---

[5]Ibid.

Mrs. Taylor was a woman filled with hidden shame. She invested most of her emotional energy in maintaining the family image. She believed that in order to be considered acceptable to others, things must always look good on the outside, even if they were terrible on the inside. She sensed the unspoken neediness in her husband, but inwardly scorned him for his weakness. She had little time to meet his emotional or sexual needs because of her endless activities. Her source of "life" was her image, and when the effort for others' approval became too great, she took to her bed with a "spell" and expected to be taken care of.

She knew that even though everyone praised her for her many church activities, the praise was really not about her as a person, but rather about her performance. Neither experiencing the fullness of God's grace in her life, nor experiencing Christ as her new identity, she had nothing to give. Shame was her identity, the only "gift" she could give to her family.

Treatment Goals for Shame

The family will need to learn the difference between shame and guilt, and the solution to each (see Chapter 11: Step Three). They will need to know that God's solution to shame is not new behaviors or more performance, but rather a new identity in Christ.

The family will need to identify the shameful messages that each person has received from the family of origin and identify what shame messages are currently operating in their family.

After family members have identified these messages, they will need to talk through feelings of anger, fear, and pain that they have experienced because of these messages.

In counseling, the family will need to learn to replace these shame messages with the truth of who they really are in God's sight. Family members will be unable to make any changes in the area of shame until they recognize the source of their shame messages and are willing to confront those messages with truth. Renewing the mind will result in the ability to choose new behaviors that correspond to an increased awareness of identity in Christ.

Perfectionism is another signal of shame in the incestuous family system. The family that projects an image of doing everything right, of keeping the peace at all costs, tends to have "living arrangements" among its members rather than real relationships. The inherent message of perfectionism is that each family member's worth is based on performance or behavior. Melanie learned very early, as do most incest victims, that trying to be perfect and "good" is one way to keep the family from falling apart and that if sexual behavior is required as the sacrifice for family harmony, then the price must be paid no matter what the cost to the child.

In counseling, each family member must identify perfectionistic behaviors that are a mask for his shame. It will be important to understand what motivated this perfectionism.

The counselor will need to assist family members to view themselves as they really are—truly weak and helpless individuals with a need to look to God for strength.

Paul, in 2 Cor. 12:9–10, states that God's grace is sufficient for each of us, that His power is made perfect in weakness. Therefore, like Paul, we can gladly admit our weaknesses so that Christ's power may rest on us; for when we are weak, then we are actually strong. Knowing the gift of God's grace, family members can learn to give themselves permission to fail, to make mistakes, to be imperfect and fallible. Experiencing their true identity and acceptance through Christ, family members can be empowered to let go of their perfectionistic, performance-oriented behaviors and allow themselves to make mistakes and still retain their self-worth.

Abuse of Power

Child sexual abuse is always an aggressive act by the perpetrator, even when there is no force or violence employed. Aggressive, rather than benevolent, use of power by the strong against the weak becomes the mode operating for all family interaction in parental incest families. Since the perpetrator and other powerful family members can be expected to continue to abuse power until they are checked, this characteristic becomes the primary family treatment need.[6]

---

[6]Susanne Sgroi, *Handbook of Clinical Intervention in Child Sexual Abuse* (Lexington, Mass.: Lexington Books, D.C. Heath and Company, 1982, D.C. Heath and Company), 251.

Power can be exercised by physical force or intimidation, as in Julie's family where her father's "suggestion" that they shower together became a "command" when she resisted. Power also can be misused by dependent/passive/weak behavior. Melanie's mother was, in actuality, a very powerful person in the family because she used frail health and fragileness to manipulate and control others.

Incestuous parents use their position of power to gratify their own needs without regard for harm done to others. Powerful individuals may rigidly demand one kind of behavior one day and, without prior notice, abandon the first expectation and substitute another.

Such misuses of power are modeled in incestuous families, teaching family members that power is important in human relationships and that powerful people can make their own rules and change them when they want. This incestuous family system uses power irresponsibly as a way to gain and maintain control.

Treatment Goals for Abusive Power

The family needs to understand how the wrong use of power has been destructive to every member of the family. Those who are abusing power must be willing to change that behavior and learn to replace aggressiveness with assertiveness. Those who have been abused must learn to become assertive rather than passive. (For assistance with assertive skills, see resources under Communication section.)

Those who hold powerful positions in the family are not going to relinquish those positions easily. In the family counseling sessions, those persons who have been abusing power may be manipulative, threatening, or aggressive in subtle ways. It is imperative that the counselor confront these behaviors:

> The therapist must convey by his or her own attitude and behavior that he or she understands how power is exercised and is able to use power in a responsible fashion. This involves confronting clients whenever they abuse power, interpreting the abusive and inappropriate aspects of their actions and refusing to back down from a stance which insists that they stop their abusive behavior and ac-

knowledge their responsibility for their actions. It requires the counselor always to behave with absolute consistency, to be unflinching in the face of hostility and threats from the client, to refuse to be manipulated, to demonstrate that he or she is willing to be held accountable and to insist that others do likewise, and unfailingly to be honest in all dealings with clients.[7]

Christ role-modeled these characteristics in His dealings with the abuse of power by the Pharisees in Matt. 23:4. Christ confronted the Pharisees, saying that they loaded the people with "impossible demands that they themselves don't even try to keep." In principle, that's what the incest offender does by placing impossible demands on his victim. The external manipulative behavior of the offender is not unlike the Pharisees, so "careful to polish the outside of the cup," leaving "the inside foul with extortion and greed" (v. 25, TLB). Denial is like "polishing the outside of the cup."

The counselor must call attention to the "inside of the cup" and disclose the wrong use of power that has used a child to meet sexual and emotional needs of the parent. Christ straightforwardly identified the blindness and hypocrisy of the Pharisees, held them accountable for their wrong behavior, was unflinching in the face of their hostility, was not manipulated by them, and yet gave them hope: "First cleanse the inside of the cup, and then the whole cup will be clean." The therapeutic balance comes from confronting wrong behavior and holding persons accountable for abusing power, but maintaining the stance that condemnation is not the issue, but rather hope and support for recovery.

Distorted Communication

Members of incestuous families do not know how to communicate with each other. In her book *Peoplemaking*, Virginia Satir compares family communication to an iceberg, and states that people in families are only aware of the "tip" of the iceberg—the small percentage that they themselves see and hear. Family members can erroneously assume that what they ob-

---

[7]Ibid., 258.

serve is all that is going on. A family's well-being relies largely on the awareness of nonverbal communication and relationship patterns that are hidden beneath the surface of everyday events.

"No-Talk" Rules

Incestuous families usually communicate indirectly or non-verbally and promote what is known as a "no-talk" rule. A no-talk rule can occasionally be verbal, but is most often a non-verbal message that certain subjects will not be discussed or even recognized as real.

In Elizabeth's family, sex was never discussed, giving the message that it was wrong to talk about. In the presence of such a no-talk rule, Uncle Phil could fondle her in the family room under a blanket while others were present in the room watching TV.

Part of the danger of no-talk rules is that a victim is left assuming others understand what is happening. For Elizabeth, the no-talk rule left her believing that her parents knew what was going on when, in fact, they did not.

The no-talk rule in incest has been likened to having an elephant in the living room: A family member announces that an elephant is in the living room, but the other members of the family look astonished and reply that there is *not* an elephant in the living room! Meanwhile, they walk around the "elephant" to avoid running into it. The purpose of the no-talk rule is, therefore, to convince the questioning family member that the incest "elephant" is not the problem, but rather that *he or she* is the problem for breaking the no-talk rule.

In Melanie's case, for example, when the incest was discovered, her mother said to her, "How could you do this to me? You have ruined the family." The incest wasn't the problem. Melanie had become the problem for saying that there was a problem.

Walking on Eggshells

Incestuous families tend to relate superficially and are "on guard" to say the right thing. Their members are preoccupied with fault and blame, and find it almost impossible to admit mistakes. Because of the heavy shame issues, and the feelings of inadequacy and defectiveness, anything that goes wrong must be someone else's fault because it is crucial to "look good" in order to protect the system from exposure.

Julie's father, for example, told her they should shower together to save water! Such hidden agendas are common, and communication is dishonest. Feelings are not dealt with straightforwardly but are denied or disregarded. Many times, certain feelings are singled out as "wrong" or "silly," and victims feel as though they are "crazy" because they are told verbally or nonverbally that their feelings are invalid or "should not" exist.

Appeasement

One of the patterns of communication in incestuous families is appeasement. The family member who appeases does not like to have others mad at him, will go along with whatever someone else wants, and will agree with others to avoid conflict whatever the cost. In addition to feeling responsible to meet the emotional needs of his stepfather, Jim felt responsible for maintaining his parents' marriage, and paid the price of silence about being sexually abused in order to avoid conflict in his family.

Blaming

Blaming, another destructive communication pattern, indicates the presence of hidden shame. To get the focus off himself and onto someone else, an incestuous father might say, "If only my wife had met my needs, I wouldn't have turned to my daughter."

When Elizabeth's mother confronted the uncle about the abuse, he insisted the incest was not his fault because Elizabeth, as a small child, ran around the house wearing only her underwear. To avoid taking responsibility for what he had done, he blamed 3-year-old Elizabeth for seducing him!

To avoid responsibility for failure to protect the child, a mother may blame the child victim for telling and thus breaking up the family. She also may blame the child for not resisting the sexual advances. When Jean reported that her mother's live-in boyfriend was abusing her, her mother responded by saying, "You got yourself into this; you get yourself out of it." The most devastating blaming, however, occurs within the child, who engages in self-blame for causing the abuse.

Controlling

Another pattern of communication in incest families is one of regimented control. The controlling person can appear very correct, unemotional, abstract, detached, or uncaring, in order to avoid facing the pain of reality. This person might resemble a computer, who presents data as intellectual and factual but without emotional expression. Often the tone of voice will be very controlled or monotone.

In her counselor's office, Sandy told of her incestuous relationship with her father, which led to her running away, walking the streets, and ultimately, engaging in prostitution. She related several beatings by her pimp that required hospitalization. Her voice was monotone and unemotional as she chronicled these traumatic events of her life in a controlled, precise and detached manner. She seemed to be speaking about someone else. The pain in her life, which began with the incest, had forced her to master the skill of controlled communication.

Confusion

The pain of reality can result in communication that is scattered, confused, and irrelevant to the current situation. A person using scattered communications will be adept at changing the subject, will tend to talk in circles, and will make statements and responses that do not make sense. Jane was abused by her stepfather for many years while receiving damaging double messages from him. He beat her and blamed her for everything that went wrong in the family, but he also told her she was a good girl because she met his sexual needs. When the abuse became known, both he and Jane's mother left town, abandoning her to an aunt. As a result of these double messages, compounded by the intense shame in her family system, her communication with others became confused and scattered. She would flit from one thought to another, monopolizing conversations by talking incessantly about self-focused trivia.

Treatment Goals for Communication Skills

The family will need to identify dysfunctional communication patterns within their family. The counselor will need to do some teaching on positive communication skills and model appropriate communication patterns. The goal for the family is to develop communication that is honest, free-flowing, and non-threatening to the self-esteem of other family members.

The family will need to learn the skill of active listening as a way of rebuilding interpersonal bridges. Active listening helps each person not only to hear the content of what someone is saying but to understand what that person's feelings are as well. This can be practiced in the counseling sessions and carried out through homework assignments in the home.

Social Isolation

Fear that someone will find out about the incest leads to isolation, one of the chief characteristics of the incestuous family. The family perceives outsiders and people in authority as hostile and avoids contact with others as much as possible. The powerful members of the family will, therefore, make sure the weaker members do not establish friendships outside the nuclear family. The family members thus receive no support, nurture, or enjoyment outside the family system.

In addition to that social isolation, individual family members are often emotionally isolated from one another, feeling lonely and hostile even before the incest occurs. They depend on each other to meet emotional and other needs. Because this type of family is unable to meet those needs, they have few outlets for the anger, tension, or aggression that is created.

In Julie's family, (Chapter 1), she and her brother lived in constant fear of her father's explosive and unpredictable anger. Because her family was so isolated, she felt she could turn to no one for help. Her rigid family, with its many unrealistic rules and expectations, remained secretive about what was going on, and provided little emotional support to one another. Each member of the family, though needy and insecure and rooted in shame, paradoxically depended on other family members for a sense of value. Even though Julie felt deep anger toward her father because he abused her and her brother, she nevertheless felt her father was her "security." She felt the family was all she had, so she endured the physical and sexual abuse for years, though she received little emotional support and felt hopelessly alone.

Melanie's family, also socially isolated, participated only in superficial and performance-based church activities that allowed an image of spirituality to be projected, thus functioning as a mask for the abuse.

Treatment Goals for Social Isolation

The family needs to look at the positive aspects of a more open family system. An open system is able to develop trusting relationships with others outside the family, able to receive support and care, and able to give each family member encouragement to take risks. The incest family will probably have a difficult time establishing trust with a counselor. It will take time, and the counselor will need to be consistent with support and care for the family.

The family members will need to identify their fears about what might happen with a more open family system. Facing these fears needs to happen in the safe and secure environment of family counseling. This process often takes a great deal of time and the counselor must give continued support.

Denial

In incestuous families, denial is used as a defense mechanism and is often the only coping skill available to family members. Susanne Sgroi observes: "Constant denial can be destructive to the individual who employs this defense mechanism because it diminishes one's capacity to empathize with others."[8] This denial robs both parents of empathy for the child victim.

It takes an enormous degree of denial for mothers to overlook incestuous behavior. One father ritualistically washed the sheets and put them away each time after abusing his daughter. His wife never asked where the clean sheets came from, who had washed them, or why.

---

[8]Ibid., 253.

Sexual abuse is so secret that those participating in it can even deny that it is happening. The father may talk about the sexual activity as "sex education" and the victim may relate to it as "helping Dad."

The effect of denial is captured in the following poem, written by a child victim in *Secret Shame: I Am a Victim of Incest*:

Danger

Danger threatened!
I knew I had to get away,
but there was no place I could go.
A girl of six
can hardly leave
the year alone.
I stayed.

Instead, I ran into my mind.
I dodged between the messages
of Mother's eyes
and Grandma's sighs—
messages which said:
don't tell the truth
we cannot bear to hear.
Cowering in the dark recesses
of an attic in my head,
I crept behind the broken furniture
of my unacceptable rage and fear.
Dust of decades,
my forbidden secret,
settled over me as I choked in guilt.
Abandoned and abused,
I sealed the doors
so that no one would know.[9]

This poem graphically describes the impact of denial on the family system. The trauma that denial inflicts on the victim is beyond measure.

---

[9]Martha Janssen, *Secret Shame: I Am a Victim of Incest* (Minneapolis: Augsburg Fortress, 1991). Reprinted by permission.

Treatment Goals for Denial

The family will need to be willing to confront the denial and go through the painful reality of the effect it has had on each person. Initially, the family may feel the need to hold on to some aspects of their denial as they begin this process. The impact of the truth can be so overwhelming that it is difficult to face all at once. The scriptural directive in John 8:32 ("You will know the truth and the truth will set you free") contains the principle that applies to this situation. The layers of denial must be removed, one at a time, in the process of facing the whole truth, in order for the family to be set free.

Lack of Intimacy

In incestuous families, intimacy is often defined solely in sexual terms. This false intimacy is a fruitless attempt to find true intimacy—being connected and sharing closely with another person in various life activities. Healthy intimacy involves closeness that is deep and personal, but in an incestuous family, the lack of trust, poor self-image, and limited ability to acknowledge and meet needs robs the family of this essential ingredient.

A primary characteristic of the incestuous family system is emotional and physical alienation between husband and wife. The husband may be angry with his wife for lack of love and intimacy in their relationship. He may abuse their child as an ultimate act of anger, communicating to his spouse that she is a worthless person, wife, and mother.

At other times, the abuse is an expression of need. A husband may act out his sense of inadequacy by seeking nurture through sexual acts with a young child. A wife may turn to a male or female child for sexual stimulation in order to satisfy deep needs for emotional security and love. She may not desire a sexual relationship with her husband because she has been a victim or because he doesn't meet her emotional needs for intimacy.

Many times, as in the Taylors' case, a wife will have illnesses, real or psychosomatic, to avoid fulfilling her role as mother and wife. As children become aware of this unspoken tension, they may fear a divorce and/or abandonment. Melanie, therefore, allowed herself to be used to keep the family system intact. In his family, Jim felt responsible to keep the marriage together by meeting needs of his stepfather that his mother was not meeting.

Treatment Goals for Intimacy

The foundation for building intimacy is trust. Members of incestuous families will need to be healed from having misplaced their trust and being hurt. The counselor or pastor may be the first person with whom they develop a trusting relationship. Trust begins to develop as each person begins to take risks and allows himself or herself to be vulnerable with others in the family during family sessions. The therapeutic relationship with a trusted counselor can be a stepping-stone to begin, or renew, a trust relationship with God.

Blurred Boundaries

Another characteristic of incest is a blurring of generational boundaries and a resultant reversal or confusion of roles. Every person has boundaries, "the invisible shield surrounding us, something like a capsule. This invisible line marks our limits— where we end and the rest of the world begins. When our boundaries are well defined, we can express and take responsibility for what we think, what we feel, and what we do."[10]

If family members deviate from their God-given roles of father, mother, child, sometimes temporarily exchanging roles, the appropriate boundaries are blurred and role confusion develops. This blurring is likely to distort every aspect of family life.

In such a family, individuals are rarely permitted to set limits for other family members in respect to their belongings, personal space, or even their own bodies. People wander into bedrooms or bathrooms, opening closed doors, walking in on others while they are taking a bath, using the bathroom, or undressing. Parents show little respect for the privacy of children: their property, bodies, and feelings. Victims learn that the word "no"

---

[10]Marilyn Mason, "Intimacy" (Center City, Minn.: Hazelden Foundation, 1986), 8.

is not allowed in their vocabulary, that refusal of a request is not an option.

In addition, powerful individuals disregard boundaries of less powerful family members, touching their belongings or their bodies. Julie's father told her she was "stupid" for feeling embarrassed when he ordered her into the shower with him, and that seeing her undressed was his right. Julie was not allowed to have any boundaries. Like Melanie and Jim, her body belonged to her father.

Another boundary violation is the allowing of opposite-sex children to share the same room or bed, or the bed of the parents. Dr. Gabriel Laury states that "faulty sleeping arrangements can represent a subtle form of sexual abuse."[11] He points out that allowing children to share a room or bed with a sibling of the opposite sex or with a parent can harm the child's psychosocial development. David Peters cautions:

> While the effects of such arrangements on a child are admittedly influenced by the age and sex of the child, the sex of the parent, and various other factors, it is a good general rule not to take such a chance in the first place. We would do well to heed the admonition of the scriptures to 'abstain from all appearances of evil' (1 Thess. 5:22, KJV). If we have any question at all about how such behavior will affect our children, we should avoid it completely.[12]

Treatment Goals for Blurred Boundaries

The family will need to be taught appropriate boundaries between family members. The counselor may use a concept from Marilyn Mason's booklet "Intimacy" as a teaching tool:

> While having boundaries or shields is important in defining ourselves, we must also be able to connect with others through the boundaries. The way we do this can be visualized as having a zipper on the inside of the shield. It can be unzipped for closeness or zipped tight for protection and withdrawal. The internal zipper can be opened when our

---

[11]David Peters, *A Betrayal of Innocence: What Everyone Should Know About Child Sexual Abuse* (Dallas, Tex.: Word Books, 1986), 34.
[12]Ibid., 35.

. . . boundary is respected, when our thoughts, feelings, and behaviors are validated and "okay."[13]

The family will need to learn appropriate roles for each member of the family—parents in parenting skills, and children as to what is appropriate for their particular age. Children need to be taught to be children, not the caretakers of their parents.

The counselor will need to assist each person to understand his motivation for playing individual roles in the family system, and what needs were being met by those roles. By clarifying boundaries and correcting reversed roles, the family can learn to meet needs in more healthy ways.

Dependency/Emotional Neediness

Because everyone has emotional needs that must be met to insure normal growth and development, each person learns to depend on some source to meet those needs. When emotional needs are not met in childhood, the child grows into a needy adult. That adult will have exaggerated dependency needs and may use pathological and destructive means, such as incest, to meet these needs for love, value, and belonging.

Scott Peck, in *The Road Less Traveled*, talks about dependency and its results:

> Passive dependency has its genesis in lack of love. The inner feeling of emptiness from which passive dependent people suffer is the direct result of their parents' failure to fulfill their children's needs for affection, attention and care during their childhood.[14]

Adults whose needs from childhood remain unmet often develop a pattern of *taking* from others, rather than giving. Even though such persons appear physically mature, they remain emotionally immature—unable to experience healthy relationships.

It is not uncommon for passive dependent people to be addicted not only to people but to drugs and alcohol as well. Theirs is the addictive personality. "They are addicted to peo-

---

[13]Mason, "Intimacy," 8.
[14]M. Scott Peck, M.D., *The Road Less Traveled* (New York: Simon and Schuster, 1978), 105.

ple, sucking on them and gobbling them up, and when people are not available to be sucked and gobbled, they often turn to the bottle, or the needle, or the pill as a people substitute."[15] Often, the dependent addictive person in the incestuous family desperately tries to meet his love needs from sources that can never fulfill—food, work, overspending, alcohol, drugs, or sex with children.

Treatment Goals for Dependency

The incestuous family's members need to learn that their love needs are valid and appropriate, but those needs must not be met at the expense of others. Family members can be taught how to more adequately meet the emotional needs of others in the family in healthy ways. They can learn to show care and concern for each other and to give appropriate physical affection.

To break the cycle of dependency, family members will need to develop individuality and an awareness of themselves as unique and valuable, apart from other family members.

Ultimately, the counselor can direct them to depend on God as the source for meeting their deep emotional needs for love and value.

Lack of Forgiveness

Without forgiveness, incest trauma will never be resolved. The concept of forgiveness is usually foreign to relationships within the incestuous family, and its suggestion is usually met with considerable resistance. Family members lower their resistance once they see the value and process of forgiveness as it relates to each individual in the family system.

The incest is like a video tape, playing and replaying the pain, resentment, hatred, or anger toward others in the family, and especially toward self. By not forgiving, victims give control of their emotional state to others. Unforgiveness allows others to control the individual's life through the constant replaying of that tape, reinforcing the pain each time it is remembered.

---

[15]Ibid., 105.

Forgiveness, however, gives a person the power to turn off the tape. Through God's grace comes the power to forgive and the power to be free from the replaying of the past.

In counseling, an incest victim will often angrily challenge the validity of forgiveness. Sara, for instance, had been a victim of physical and sexual abuse by her father for 10 years and was consumed with rage toward him. With clenched fists and reddened face, she shouted, "Are you trying to tell me that I have to forgive my father?" As she continued venting her rage, the real issue emerged in this statement: "If I forgive my father, that means what he did to me was okay."

Such misconceptions about forgiveness are common. A prevalent misconception, as illustrated in Sara's story, is that forgiveness means saying that what happened is now forgotten. The purpose of forgiving, however, is not to forget the events, but to stop the tape from continuing to replay the lingering pain. Too often, victims are told to "forgive and forget," and that if they have not forgotten the abuse, they have not truly forgiven.

Another misconception is that family members should excuse the wrong behavior because the molester was "sick" or drunk, or because his wife didn't meet his needs. In truth, forgiving does not make excuses for wrong. Individuals must be held accountable for the full extent of their behavior.

Another misunderstanding is that forgiveness means we are called to be peacemakers who should not cause conflict by talking about the abuse. Some have reinforced this concept by using Eph. 5:12: "For it is shameful even to mention what the disobedient do in secret." However, verse 11, immediately before, and verse 13, following, admonish us to "expose deeds of darkness" so that in the light they will become "visible." True forgiveness can occur only in the light of truth, not in the suppression of it.

Many times families are re-victimized by another invalid idea about forgiveness: If they "truly" forgive, they will "trust" each other implicitly. But forgiveness is a process, and trust must be rebuilt after betrayal. In cases where family members have taken full responsibility to change their behavior, trusting might be an appropriate response. But, in many cases, forgiveness is just a word that is exchanged without any accompanying evidence of personal responsibility to change.

This was the case for Sam, who consented to meet with his pastor when Sam's wife discovered his incestuous behavior with their 6-year-old daughter. After meeting with the pastor, Sam came home, asked his daughter for forgiveness, and told his wife everything had been dealt with. Sam's wife called the pastor to request further counseling for her and her daughter. He told her Sam had repented and asked forgiveness, and she should now forgive him and trust him. Trusting Sam at this point led to his abuse of his daughter again within six months.

Asking for forgiveness is not simply saying "I'm sorry." Remorse may be nothing more than regret over being caught. Repentance is true grief over the pain the behavior has caused, and a change in behavior.

Treatment Goals for Lack of Forgiveness

To begin the forgiveness process, each family member needs to evaluate the full impact of the incest on him or her personally. Family members will be unable to forgive that which has not been completely identified. It will be critical to the forgiving process that the family members not be allowed to minimize their pain or rationalize their behavior.

The counselor will need to help them separate reality from fantasy, especially fantasies like "it's not that bad" or "this really didn't happen." It will also be necessary to assess the areas that need forgiveness, such as broken trust, emotional and/ or physical trauma, humiliation, and shattered self-image.

Important to the forgiveness process is the understanding that it *is* a process, not a one-time choice of the will. The counselor will need to give the family permission to express any and all feelings openly and honestly to each other, especially anger and resentment. Scripture encourages this in Eph. 4:25: "Therefore, each of you must put off falsehood and speak truthfully . . . for we are all members of one body." Putting off falsehood is more than simply telling the truth. It involves removing masks and "layers" of protection so that relationships can develop. For families who have never done this, this can seem to be a monumental task. It is not uncommon for family members to rush into asking forgiveness, or express forgiveness to each other, before they have processed the underlying pain. This premature expression of forgiveness may be motivated by a desire to do the "right" thing, or to have everything "over with" because the situation is so intensely painful for the entire family.

David Augsburger writes:

> Forgiveness, which is a complex and demanding process, is often reduced to a single act of accepting another. In spite of the pain, hurt, loss, and wrongdoing that stand between us, we are encouraged to forgive in a single act of resolving all by giving unconditional inclusion. Such a step becomes too large for any human to take in a single bound. Forgiveness is a journey of many steps, each of which can be extremely difficult, all of which are to be taken carefully, thoughtfully, and with deep reflection.[16]

To facilitate forgiveness, each family member will benefit by seeing the counselor individually to help each person identify his feelings, then write out those feelings. Each will need to prepare to express those feelings verbally, first to the counselor, and then to other family members. The counselor needs to warn the family members that strong emotional feelings will be aroused, and they may experience a great deal of painful intensity, anger, and crying. Each person must be reassured that he should not be ashamed for having these feelings nor try to hold them in.

The counselor plays a key role in discerning the right timing for the family to come together to express their feelings. Sharing with family members should come only when the counselor feels that the members are strong enough to stand up against powerful individuals in the family and that the stronger members will not inflict further pain on the weaker ones. The last step in the process is to say, "I forgive you." A great deal of time may need to elapse between the expression of honest feelings and the "I forgive you."

Most families will experience barriers to forgiveness, such as holding on to negative behaviors out of a fear of change or wanting others to feel sorry for them and wanting to be taken care of. Often a barrier to forgiveness is wanting to pay back

---

[16]David Augsburger, *Caring Enough to Forgive* (Ventura, Calif.: Regal Books, 1981), 30.

those who have hurt them, or fearing being hurt again. A common barrier to complete forgiveness is feeling able to forgive others but being unable to forgive self and accept God's forgiveness. None of these responses are unusual, and most have been used as survival skills. It will be important for the counselor to model God's grace and supportive love to encourage each family member to "put off" the old, negative behavior patterns "and to put on the new self created to be like God in true righteousness and holiness" (Eph. 4:22–24). (For specific tools to facilitate the process of forgiveness in adult victims, see Step Seven.)

Characteristics of Incestuous Families
1. Shame
2. Abuse of power
3. Distorted communication
4. Social isolation
5. Denial
6. Lack of intimacy
7. Blurred boundaries
8. Dependency/emotional neediness
9. Lack of forgiveness

Recommended Resources:

Allender, Dan. "Shame: What It Means to Fear Exposure," *Institute of Biblical Counseling Perspective.* (A publication of the Institute of Biblical Counseling, Winona Lake, Indiana, 1985).

Augsburger, David. *Caring Enough to Forgive.* Ventura, Calif.: Regal Books, 1981.

Fossum, Merle and Marilyn Mason. *Facing Shame: Families in Recovery.* N.Y.: W.W. Norton and Co., 1986.

Frank, Jan. *A Door of Hope,* San Bernardino, Calif.: Here's Life Publishers, 1987.

Halpern, Howard M. *How To Break Your Addiction to a Person.* Toronto, Ontario, Canada: Bantam Books, 1982.

Hancock, Maxine and Karen, Mains. *Child Sexual Abuse: A Hope for Healing.* Wheaton, Ill.: Harold Shaw Publishers, 1987. See Chapter 6.

Kaufman, Gershen. *Shame: The Power of Caring.* Cambridge, Mass.: Schenkman Publishing Co., 1980.

Mason, Marilyn. "Intimacy." Center City, Minn.: Hazelden Foundation, 1986.

Martin, Grant L. *Counseling for Family Violence and Abuse.* Dallas, Tex.: Word Books, 1987.

Needham, David C. *Birthright: Christian, Do You Know Who You Are?* Portland, Ore.: Multnomah Press, 1979. A resource to help combat shame by enhancing understanding of our identity in Christ.

Norwood, Robin. *Women Who Love Too Much.* N.Y.: Simon and Schuster, 1985.

Peck, M. Scott, M.D. *The Road Less Traveled.* N.Y.: Simon and Schuster, 1978.

Seamands, David. *Healing Grace.* Wheaton, Ill.: Victor Books, 1988.

Seamands, David. *Healing for Damaged Emotions.* Wheaton, Ill.: Victor Books, 1985. See Chapters 7–9.

Smedes, Lewis. *Forgive and Forget: Healing the Hurts We Don't Deserve.* N.Y.: Harper and Row, 1984.

VanVonderen, Jeff. *Tired of Trying to Measure Up*, Minneapolis: Bethany House Publishers, 1989.

VanVonderen, Jeff. "Wounded by Shame; Healed by Grace." Tape series from Damascus, Inc., P.O. Box 22432, Minneapolis, MN 55422.

Whitaker, Carl and Augustus, Napier. *The Family Crucible.* N.Y.: Harper and Row, 1978.

Wilson, Earl D. *A Silence to Be Broken.* Portland, Ore.: Multnomah Press, 1986. See Chapter 7.

Woititz, Janet. *The Struggle for Intimacy.* Deerfield Beach, Fla.: Health Communications, Inc., 1985.

Wright, H. Norman. *Making Peace With Your Past.* Old Tappan, N.J.: Fleming H. Revell Company, 1985. See Chapter 7.

Sexual Abuse Offenders: Brethren, This Ought Not to Be . . .

Brad Smyth, a dentist, faithfully attends his church and belongs to a nationally known Christian evangelism and discipleship ministry. He appears to be a normal, loving father of a close-knit family.

Those who think they know him, however, have not seen what God has seen in that family. Behind closed doors, Brad fondles 11-year-old Karen's breasts and forces her to "practice" kissing him. She feels very uncomfortable and afraid of what her father is doing, but he ignores her attempts to stop him. This week, Brad became so forceful in his advances that he pushed Karen down onto her bed while she cried and screamed and tried to push him away. Four-year-old Brian stood by Karen's bed, hitting his father with his teddy bear and sobbing, "Daddy, stop! Daddy, stop!"

Can Christians Be Sex Offenders?

The grievous fact is that child sexual abuse is practiced by many professing Christians. Unfortunately many believers are unprepared to confront the myths that perpetuate our denial. Some insist the issue of sexual abuse should not be discussed because it *should not* and, therefore, *does not* happen among Christians. These people feel that talk of abuse is wrong and may even encourage it to happen. Their perspective denies the existence of the problem and does not look at reality.

However, even an honest facing of this issue can lead to error. One perspective views the Christian sex offender as having a spiritual problem that can be corrected solely by spiritual exercises, such as reading the Bible or prayer. Another perspective views that same offender as having psychological problems that can be helped only through psychiatric intervention outside of the church. In the authors' experience, however, Christians sometimes *are* sex offenders, and the solution to the problem involves both spiritual and psychological perspectives, rather than either perspective alone.

Spiritual Influences: The World, the Flesh and the Devil

Although Christians are not to be "conformed to this world" (Rom. 12:2), we, nonetheless, can be influenced by it. As David Peters writes: "The world affects both Christians and non-Christians in a number of different ways. Entertainment, advertising, peer pressures, educational systems, and prevailing philosophies are only a few of the influences affecting the beliefs and behaviors of people."[1] The worldly influences that contribute to alcoholism, drug addiction, and pornography are often factors that trigger sexual abuse. The *National Federation for Decency Journal* reported that *"Penthouse* magazine claims that 35% of its readers are born-again Christians. The pornographic magazine claims to have 1.67 million born-again readers . . ."[2] For many Christians, these statistics may be hard to believe. Many people within the church are sheltered from such experiences and understandably find it difficult to comprehend a Christian brother or sister struggling with such influences in the world. Nevertheless, those of us within the church remain responsible before God to open our eyes and see the reality of these struggles within the body of Christ.

While the world system is an *external* influence, we must be aware, as Peters notes, of "the *internal* influence which the flesh and lust have on human moral choices."[3] God desires believers to make moral choices that reflect their identity in Christ, rather than fleshly desires. James 1:14–15 points out the importance of personal responsibility: "But each one is being so-

---

[1] David B. Peters, *A Betrayal of Innocence: What Everyone Should Know About Child Sexual Abuse* (Dallas, Tex.: Word Books, 1986), 27.
[2] *National Federation for Decency Journal* (Feb. 1987), 15.
[3] Peters, *A Betrayal of Innocence*, 29.

licited to sin when he is taken in tow and enticed by his own craving. Then when the aforementioned craving has conceived, it gives birth to sin, and this sin, when it is full grown, brings forth death."[4] Death in this context does not refer primarily to physical death, but to spiritual and emotional separation from God and others. If the offender allows the temptation of the flesh, accompanied by lust, to gain control of him, sexual abuse can result.

Satan is described in Scripture as "the god of this world,"[5] although much of his power comes from society's unbelief in his existence. In 1 Pet. 5:8, we are advised to "be of a sober mind, be watchful. Your adversary, who is a slanderer, namely, the devil, as a lion roaring in fierce hunger, is constantly walking about, always seeking someone to be devouring."[6] Some of Satan's most devastating forces are aimed at the destruction of children and families, which would seem to be his ultimate affront to God. One must not underestimate the spiritual battle for the mind, will, and emotions of the person who has fallen into sexual sin with children.

The spiritual impact of the world, the flesh, and the Devil needs to be examined in the life of the offender who professes to be a Christian. Such personal examination will need to take into consideration specific world views and philosophies, such as self-gratification, use of pornography, and other influences in the worldly system that contributed to the abusive behavior. The offender who professes to be a Christian must look at the foundation from which moral choices are made. Succumbing to the temptation of lust, which is then acted out sexually with children, signals to the Christian that the flesh has become the source of fulfillment rather than God. This introspection will lead to an awareness of those areas in which Satan has gained access into the life of that individual. Such examination will be a significant part of the recovery process for the offender, the victim and the family.

---

[4]Kenneth S. Wuest, *The New Testament: An Expanded Translation* (Grand Rapids: William B. Eerdmans Publishing Co., 1978), 540.
[5]2 Corinthians 4:4, RSV.
[6]Wuest, *The New Testament: An Expanded Translation*, 558.

Psychological Influences

Several psychological traits are common to most types of offenders. It is a well-known fact that most sex offenders were physically and/or sexually abused as children. Low self-esteem and deep feelings of inadequacy are almost always key factors that motivate abusers to meet their needs in an unhealthy way. If, added to these, the individual struggles with a sense of alienation or isolation from others and a feeling of being a helpless victim in an overpowering environment, then the groundwork is laid for a need to exert power over others to "prove" self-worth. This frustrated need for power and control, coupled with inability to delay immediate gratification of sexual needs, could combine to be the final factors in influencing a person to sexually abuse children. Often offenders have little insight into their own behavior, and thus may be very insensitive and unaware of the needs of others. This insensitivity is often reflected in their inability to perceive the harm and the pain they are causing their victims. Their rigid defense system of denial and rationalization can dull their conscience to the point that they do not perceive that what they are doing is wrong.

Kevin's story illustrates many of these factors that led to the sexual abuse of his 5-year-old cousin. Kevin was raised in a large family of 10 children, with parents who had been previously divorced before marrying each other. He felt lost in the crowd of sisters and brothers and found it hard to make friends. He was physically abused by older cousins and stepbrothers who resented the marriage, and he felt unable to protect himself. His stepfather would shame him and tell him he was a "wimp" because he wouldn't fight back. His stepfather told Kevin he needed to "grow up and be a man" and initiated him into "manhood" by forcing Kevin into mutual masturbation with him.

This sexual abuse began a cycle of compulsive masturbation in Kevin's life. At age 13, he became involved in reading pornographic magazines and was obsessed with his sexual needs. He felt that he had no respect from his family members and considered himself powerless to escape from his brothers. Kevin also felt powerless to control his compulsive masturbation and hated himself for not being able to stop.

In the midst of Kevin's inner conflict, he was asked to babysit for his 5-year-old cousin, Rhonda. She looked up to Kevin as a big brother and friend and enjoyed his special attention. He felt accepted and loved by her, and for the first time in his life, he was in control of a relationship. Because Rhonda trusted him, he was able to gain power over her to the point that she was willing to do whatever he asked her to do. He enjoyed the feeling of her willingness to do special favors for him.

Kevin's neediness, his desire for control, his preoccupation with his sexual desires, together with the vulnerability of his cousin, set the stage for sexual abuse. In the exhilaration of the initial sexual contact, Kevin felt fulfilled as never before. Increasingly, he turned to her to meet the emptiness that had never been filled. He was blinded to the damage that he was causing in Rhonda's life. He felt that being sexual with his cousin was just part of their total relationship and, therefore, would not admit to himself that it was wrong.

Many of the factors in Kevin's story are common to most types of sex offenders. It is possible, however, to identify several distinct types of sex offenders.

Adolescent Offenders

As an adolescent, Kevin represents a large percentage of sex offenders, most of whom are male. The adolescent sex offender may be the boy next door. He is typically a nice quiet young man, a loner who keeps to himself. He is usually an average or above average student who is often appreciated by his teachers because of his pleasing behavior. He is usually isolated from peers, has a low self-esteem, and a history of abuse, usually sexual. Because he does not have friends who take up his time and because he is quiet and well behaved, he is often asked to babysit for small children. His victims are usually fond of him and will participate in sexual activities for long periods of time before the secret about the abuse comes out. If the children do tell about the abuse, they may not be believed because he is such a "nice guy."

In the past, teenagers who committed acts of sexual abuse were thought to be awkward explorers of their emerging sexuality. Abusive acts were dismissed as misguided sexual experimentation or developmental anomalies—the "boys will be boys" rationalization—by professionals interested in protecting adolescents from social stigmatization.

Some recent studies, however, suggest that adolescent sexual offenders represent a serious social problem. Not only do they commit a relatively large number of sexual crimes (in 1983, juveniles accounted for 40% of the total arrests for sexual offenses excluding prostitution in St. Paul, Minn.), but these often represent the early stages of a developing sexual deviance that the adolescent carries into adult life.[7]

A study was conducted that revealed the prevalence of teenage sex offenders who continued to offend well into their adult life:

> After securing a federal guarantee of immunity from prosecution for respondents, they interviewed over 350 sex offenders, many of whom had never been prosecuted. Over half had committed their first sexual crimes before they were 18 years of age. Child molesters who were attracted primarily to young boys had the earliest onset: 53% reported deviant arousal patterns by age 15, and 74% by age 19. More alarming still was the finding that those offenders who began their sexual victimization "careers" in the teenage years committed an average of 380 sexual crimes by the time they were interviewed as adults.[8]

There are several types of adolescents who sexually abuse, and many different motivations behind their abusive behavior. The following types illustrate some of the general categories of adolescent sex offenders, but is not intended as an all-inclusive definition. Some treatment issues are discussed, but these should only be viewed as a brief summary of the treatment process.

The "Experimenter"

Some adolescent sex offenders are naively experimenting with their newly developing sexuality and commit a few iso-

---

[7]Michael O'Brien and Walter Bera, "Adolescent Sexual Offenders: A Descriptive Typology," *Preventing Sexual Abuse*, vol. 1, no. 3, (Fall 1986), 1.
[8]Ibid., 2.

lated events of sexual exploration with young children, usually between the ages of 2 and 6.[9] This experimenting offender needs appropriate sex education and teaching about his own sexuality. He will need to take responsibility for the sexual abuse and its implications for him and his victim. The family will need to develop more open communication about sexuality.

The "Loner"

Another type of adolescent offender is the loner, who feels isolated from family and peers. This adolescent is usually a member of a dependent family system and may be placed in more of a parent role than a child's role in that family. He will typically abuse, without force or threats, to meet his emotional needs for intimacy and self-esteem. This adolescent would benefit from individual and group counseling to address the issues of self-esteem, sexuality, and responsibility for the abuse; and family counseling to address areas of role reversal, dependency issues, and assertive communication skills.

The "Boy Next Door"

There are other adolescent offenders, often older, who have good social skills and are high achievers, with little or no history of "acting out" behavior. This boy-next-door type of offender was probably a victim of early childhood abuse or neglect and becomes self-centered and devoted to the pursuit of meeting his own personal needs at others' expense. He seems to be narcissistic and uses children strictly for his sexual pleasure without regard to the impact on his victim. He usually abuses over a longer period of time and appears to have little remorse or guilt. This type of adolescent offender, without intervention, is very likely to develop a lifelong pattern of sexually abusing children. He may be poorly motivated to change and will require long-term treatment. It may take a great deal of time to break through his denial and rationalization system. He will need to take responsibility to stop hurting *others,* which demonstrates true repentance, rather than stopping the abuse because it's getting

---

[9]Ibid., 2.

him into trouble, which only demonstrates remorse over getting caught.

The "Aggressor"

Another type of adolescent offender uses aggression and/or violence to accompany his abuse.

> Troy, age 15, was a victim of severe physical abuse at the hands of his stepfather, his mother's third husband. The mother was passive and often suffered from physical beatings from her husband as well. Troy had a history of firesetting, theft, vandalism and truancy over several years.
>
> Very social and flamboyant, he took a 14-year-old girl out on a date and when she refused to "go all the way," Troy slapped her and forced her to perform oral sex by threatening her with a screwdriver.
>
> Sexual aggressors are typically products of disorganized and abusive families. They have good peer age social skills and are often charming and gregarious. Typically, having a long history of anti-social behaviors and poor impulse control problems, they often fight with family members and friends and are likely to abuse chemicals. The sexual abuse typically involves the use of forced threats or violence. The victims can be peers, adults or children. Psychological testing usually reveals an anti-social and character-disordered teenager. The offender's motivation for abuse is the use of sex to experience personal power through domination, express anger, or humiliate his victim. In more extreme cases, there may actually be a learned sexual arousal to violence itself so that violence alone becomes sexually arousing and the expression of violence enhances the pleasure of a sex act.[10]

Because of the dysfunctional family system, it will be difficult for this type of offender to make significant and lasting changes in his behavior. This family is likely to try to sabotage his treatment goals because of the impact family counseling will have on their family system. This character-disordered adolescent most often requires residential long-term treatment to learn

---

[10]Ibid., 3.

appropriate ways to express anger, to work through his own abuse issues, and to take responsibility for his abuse of others. This offender will not change unless he is able to truly repent over his wrong behavior.

The "Group" Offender

Another type of adolescent may not sexually abuse on his own, but might become involved in abuse as a result of pressure in a group situation, especially if the leader of the group was one of the previously described types of sex offenders. In the case of a group sex offense, each of the offenders must be held individually accountable for his actions, rather than allowed to blame others for his involvement. In counseling, he will need to look at areas causing vulnerability to peer pressure and at ways to reduce that vulnerability to outside influence. This offender will need to address issues of self-esteem and assertiveness versus aggressiveness.

Adolescent Female Offenders

Just as victims can be male or female, it is also important to be aware that adolescent sex offenders can be male or female. One mother observed her 3-year-old son lying on top of her 18-month-old daughter. When she asked her son what he was doing, he replied, "I'm making honey like the babysitter does." The parents were able to piece together the events to realize that the 13-year-old female babysitter had been sexually abusing their son and calling it the "making honey" game.

Thirteen is the average age of the adolescent female offender, with over half of the offenses involving children under the age of four.[11] It is more common for female adolescents to offend once or twice and then stop because they have a tendency to think more about how their victim feels or what others would think of them if they knew. In the authors' experience, it is not an uncommon occurrence to have female members in a support group for victims of sexual abuse to share how they, too, had

---

[11]Paula Lantz, "Characteristics of Female Adolescent Sex Offenders—Some Research Results" (Bloomington, Minn.: *Treating the Juvenile Sexual Abuse Perpetrator: A National Training Conference*, April 27–30, 1986).

sexually victimized a young child during their adolescence. On those occasions, when a female victim reveals that she herself had abused a child, she will most often need to work through issues in overcoming shame for committing a crime for which, she feels, there is no forgiveness, either from God or from others. She will need to take full responsibility for the sexual abuse and for its impact on the victim. She also needs appropriate sex education regarding her own sexuality.

Adult Fixated Offenders

Adult fixated offenders are defined as pedophiles. A pedophile is a man, or occasionally a woman, who receives emotional, psychological and sexual gratification from children. "Almost half of fixated offenders were victims of child sexual abuse, usually victimized by a non-family member in a violent manner. And from this, the message begins: 'The world is a cruel and demanding place, void of love from adults.'[12] Whether the offender was sexually abused as a child or not, his family system was dysfunctional, leaving him with feelings of sadness and loneliness and an emptiness he tries to fill with his involvement with children. He may even believe that by being a "special friend" to his victim, he is giving the child something he never had as a child.

In order to understand this type of sex offender, we need to look at the abuse from his perspective. This person is threatened by adult relationships, which seem to him to be very demanding. To try to get the most care and nurturing for himself, he chooses relationships with children, who make very few demands. From his perspective, the more the child is sexually involved with him, the more he feels the child is committed to the relationship and, therefore, the more the child "loves" him. From the distorted perspective of the pedophile, he sees the child as not only being his equal, but as actually being more powerful in the relationship. He fears rejection by the child and often will try to keep the child in the relationship by pleasing the child and giving the child anything he or she wants.

---

[12]Linda Tschirhart Sanford, *The Silent Children: A Parent's Guide to the Prevention of Child Sexual Abuse* (New York: McGraw-Hill Book Company, 1982), 101.

Many times the offender is emotionally immature and irre-sponsible to the point that he will do anything to coerce the child into remaining in the relationship. He even rationalizes that because of his "love" for the child, he is powerless to con-trol his own behavior, as illustrated in the following statement from a 31-year-old offender: "I really loved this kid—not just for his body—but really just for him. He told me to get the money for the minibike, or he'd leave me. So I stole to get it. What else could I do?"[13]

"Sometimes he molests a child only once . . . as did an oth-erwise exemplary Boy Scout leader who molested one of his charges on an overnight camping trip. More often, however, the pedophile seeks a long-term, loving relationship with a child . . . as (in the case of) the single adult male who adopted a young-ster and subsequently molested him over a period of years."[14]

Pedophiles may be single or in a marriage of convenience. The majority of them are over 18,[15] and almost all pedophiles (about 99%) tend to be passive, lonely men. "Only about 1% are sadists who cruelly assault their victims through rape and torture."[16] There is usually no history of addiction to alcohol or drugs, but they are instead addicted to sexual behavior with children. "Some incestuous fathers engage in extrafamilial pe-dophilic acts. In these cases, the fathers are classified as pedo-philes because their primary orientation appears to be toward children in general and not just toward their own offspring."[17] Fixated offenders are usually immature in their social skills, and tend to avoid relationships with adults while seeking out children to meet their social and sexual needs.

Almost half of all pedophiles use their occupation as a major access route to child victims. The adult pedophile who has an authority position in the lives of children is often able to survey a child's family history to assess that child's vulnerability to his advances. The pedophile who uses his role as a means to impose authority and control on a child may be in such authority po-

---

[13]Sanford, *The Silent Children*, 103.

[14]Adele Mayer, *Sexual Abuse: Cause, Consequences and Treatment of Inces-tuous and Pedophilic Acts* (Holmes Beach, Fla.: Learning Publications, Inc., 1985), 20.

[15]Ibid., 21.

[16]Ibid., 20.

[17]Ibid., 21.

sitions as teacher, city health officer, school bus driver, Sunday school teacher, camp counselor, or scout leader.

Sometimes an adult's status in the neighborhood helps to legitimize his presence with children and their parents and permits unquestioned exchange of young people in and out of his home. Often such a person is well liked by many of his neighbors. He usually has befriended and interacted closely only with those neighbors who have children of the sex and age that he prefers. In some cases, he may be willing to develop such a friendship for years while waiting for a neighbor's child to reach his age preference.

> The offender can show incredible patience in his premeditation of the crime as he waits to be accepted as "one of the guys." States a 28-year-old offender:
> "I got busted for molesting these boys on my baseball team. But it wasn't like I was exploiting them; I'd worked with those kids for a full year on nothing but their batting and fielding before I ever molested them. It took me that long before they trusted me and stopped treating me like a tough adult coach."[18]

The pedophile exploits children in different ways to get them to participate in sexual acts. One way is enticement, in which the offender attempts to seduce the child through persuasion, as Jim's father did when he took Jim on camping trips and did special things with him to earn his favor. Other enticements could be bribes and rewards such as money, gifts, treats, good times, and/or affection. Receiving such rewards makes the child feel obligated to the offender, setting him up for the next step of exploitation. The offender then entraps the child by taking advantage of his or her feelings of obligation. In Jim's case, Jim was set up to feel responsible to meet his father's sexual needs because of all his father had done for him. Once the child has been victimized, the offender may use threats or blackmail to maintain control.

Regressed Adult Offenders

The regressed offender tends to revert to being sexual with children when he is experiencing some extreme stress in his

---

[18]Sanford, *The Silent Children*, 103.

life. Prior to this time, his sexual interest and social activities were focused on those his own age. Regressed offenders are drawn to children in an attempt to replace the loss of an adult relationship that was meaningful, or to compensate for another significant loss in life. Such losses might be a deterioration of a marriage, illness or death of a spouse, a spouse working odd hours or being away from home. Aging can be a stress that precipitates sexual abuse. An elderly offender might be reacting to the loss of sexual functioning, retirement, or death of a spouse and/or friends.

Financial loss was a major stress that occurred in the life of John Jones, who was an elder in his church. He began sexually abusing his adolescent male foster children in response to the crushing blow of his business failure. The crisis of bankruptcy made him feel inadequate, a failure as a provider for his family, and filled with anger because he felt he had no control over the situation. When the frustration and anger of his wife added to his feelings of failure and inadequacy, he turned to his foster sons to meet his emotional and sexual needs.

The regressed offender is usually married or in a common-law, live-in situation. Female victims are his primary target, and sexual contact with the child co-exists with sexual contact with adults. In many cases, the offense will occur when the offender is using alcohol. Alcohol does not cause the abuse, but is thought to remove inhibitions within the offender which then allows the abuse to occur. The first episode of sexual contact is often an impulsive act. Unlike the fixated offender, the initial act is not usually premeditated.

Most regressed offenders are involved in incest. Susanne Sgroi, in her *Handbook of Clinical Intervention in Child Sexual Abuse,* states that in her clinical experience, she has "found that in fact the majority—an estimated 90%—of incest offenders fall into this category."[19] Sgroi notes that incestuous fathers often have feelings of inadequacy and are unsure of themselves in handling the adult stresses of marriage and parenthood. An incestuous father may respond in one of two ways. He may either choose a passive-dependent withdrawal from his role in

---

[19]Susanne Sgroi, *Handbook of Clinical Intervention in Child Sexual Abuse* (Lexington, Mass.: Lexington Books, D.C. Heath and Company, 1982, D.C. Heath and Company), 218.

the family and, like a child, expect others to take care of him and meet his needs. The incest relationship then becomes a substitute for his marriage relationship. Or, he may become overly controlling and a rigid authoritarian to prove that he is "in charge." The incest relationship provides a means of exerting control and bolstering his feelings of adequacy. "For both types of offenders, the passive-dependent-submissive type and the aggressive-controlling-dominant type, the incest behavior is a precarious and unsuccessful attempt to compensate for or replace a feeling of loss or deprivation."[20]

This clinical picture points to an underlying issue of shame. The incest offender is but one more example of an "empty" person, void of experiencing the fullness of Christ, who turns to another to meet his needs for love, value and significance. In the case of incest, the sins of the father affect the children and are passed on from generation to generation.[21]

Treatment Goals for Adult Pedophiles

When considering treatment for adult sex offenders, one must decide which offenders are suitable for treatment and what type of treatment will be most beneficial. The following treatment goals provide a brief summary of the issues that need to be addressed with the sexual abuse offender. These guidelines can be used for evaluation and assist in making appropriate referrals. The clinical evaluation of the offender needs to address the risk of the offender repeating his offense, whether he poses a threat to the victim, whether he is receptive to treatment, and whether in- or out-patient treatment is most appropriate. The counselor will need to assess the offender's personality functioning, communication skills, ability to think rationally, and ability to respond appropriately and adapt to the stress of life situations. He must be willing to take full responsibility for the offense, admit his wrongdoing, be concerned about the damage the abuse has caused the victim, and be truly repentant for what he has done.

There is a poor prognosis for recovery in an offender whose personality is characterized by lifelong ingrained maladaptive

---

[20]Ibid., 225.
[21]Exodus 34:6–7, NIV.

behavior. This type of offender seems to have an inability to learn from his past experiences or punishments. Although he may appear outwardly charming, he is a master at manipulating others and using them for his own purpose. He uses basic defense mechanisms of blaming others, denying his own actions and how those actions have affected others, and rationalizing why he committed the offense.

If an offender displays the following characteristics or behaviors, he may only be suitable for in-patient programs that are found in psychiatric hospitals and prisons:

Psychological Patterns	*Behavioral Patterns*
1. Absence of guilt or remorse	1. Using violence
2. Low tolerance for frustration	2. Using sadism
	3. Record of sexual offenses
3. Inability to tolerate criticism/confrontation	4. Sexually addictive behavior, especially sexual deviancy beginning in adolescence
4. Chronic sexual fixation on children, especially male children	
5. Inability to be empathetic	

Offenders who are not exhibiting the above characteristics may be appropriate for a community-based, out-patient program. Even though offenders may be appropriate for treatment, they may not choose to attend unless they are ordered to do so by the court. The offender's sexual offense is not only a symptom of his spiritual condition and psychological dysfunction, it is also a crime and it must be dealt with on multiple levels. This will require criminal justice intervention as well as a social service intervention, working in conjunction with the church.

Traditionally, the church has wanted to handle conflicts of the family or of church members within the setting of the congregation. However, in the case of sex offenders, in addition to breaking God's laws, they have broken civil law. We are directed by Rom. 13:1–2 to submit such crimes to our civil authorities: "Everyone must submit himself to the governing authorities, for there is no authority except that which God has established. The authorities that exist have been established by God. Consequently, he who rebels against the authority is rebelling against what God has instituted, and those who do so will bring judgment on themselves." Verse 5 continues: "Therefore, it is necessary to submit to the authorities, not only because of possible punishment but also because of conscience."[22]

While reporting to civil authorities those church members who have committed sex offenses is a sad and difficult duty, it is necessary to remember that God is ultimately in control over those civil authorities because He has ordained them. To maintain a clear conscience before God, we must trust that even though reporting seems to create a more difficult situation for the offender, the victim, and the families involved, the fact is that, ultimately, reporting provides a significant opportunity for intervention and restoration.

Many times in sexual abuse cases, Christians feel they should protect those involved from facing even more shame and rejection through exposure within the church and in the community. By not reporting the abuse, however, Christians demonstrate a lack of trust in God's ability to work all things out ". . . for the good of those who love Him"[23] and those who look to Him for help.

In the case of Mark and Mary Hanson, reporting the abuse of their 3-year-old daughter proved to be a situation that produced positive results. The Hansons' 12-year-old neighbor boy, Jeff, had taken a particular interest in their daughter, Lisa.

One night, after Jeff had been babysitting, Mrs. Hanson found the guest room bed unmade and she questioned her children about it. Lisa told her mother that Jeff had told her older brothers to go watch TV while Jeff took Lisa into the guest bedroom to play "where babies come from." Further questioning revealed that Jeff had removed Lisa's clothes and fondled her, under the pretense of teaching her this new "game."

Mr. Hanson was appalled when he first heard about the abuse. He had often befriended Jeff and felt betrayed. He was counseled by his pastor to report the abuse to child protection services, but he at first refused. He knew Jeff's father was already abusive to his son and he feared further retribution for both

---

[22]Romans 13:1–2, 5, NIV.
[23]Romans 8:28, NIV.

himself and Jeff if he disclosed the truth. The Hansons got into a family argument about whether or not to report the abuse. Mrs. Hanson wanted to call the authorities right away, while Mr. Hanson felt she was overreacting, that Jeff was only 12 and was just going through some adolescent experimentation. Mr. Hanson had been sharing his faith with Jeff and felt that if he reported the abuse, it would damage their relationship.

Mr. Hanson's pastor reassured him that reporting the abuse and getting Jeff some help was the way to show real care for Jeff. Reluctantly, Mr. Hanson called child protection and reported the abuse. After talking with Lisa, a protection worker confronted both Jeff and his parents about the seriousness of the abuse. The Hansons then took the opportunity to meet with Jeff and his parents at their home. The Hansons told Jeff he would no longer be allowed to babysit their daughter, that he needed to tell their daughter that he had been wrong to play that "game," that he was sorry about what he had done, and that it would not happen again.

Even though the Hansons felt angry and betrayed by the incident, and they were appropriately protective of Jeff's further contact with their daughter, they still desired to show care to Jeff. Mr. Hanson took Jeff out fishing, as he had promised he would do before he had learned about the abuse. Once the abuse was reported, Jeff's family was required to receive counseling. Mr. and Mrs. Hanson, along with Lisa, also sought out a counselor who specialized in abuse counseling.

Because of the pastor's faithfulness in educating his congregation about issues such as sexual abuse, the Hansons were equipped with some basic skills in handling this crisis. They also were aware of the distinction between confronting Jeff's wrong behavior and yet ministering to Jeff as a needy young boy. In the Hansons' case, their situation was worked out for the good, but while the Hansons' case is shared as an encouragement to trust the reporting process, it is important to recognize that not every case will bear such favorable results.

Another area of hesitancy for Christians is counseling for sex offenders provided outside the church. Even though there may be valid conflicts in treatment philosophies, in the absence of a Christian alternative, the offender can benefit from a secular program with the assistance of a knowledgeable and equipped support system within his church that supplements the treatment program where it lacks appropriate spiritual dimensions. One secular program in Minnesota[24] contains many positive components in the treatment of adolescent sex offenders, which are amenable to Christian ideology. The program requires the offender to take full responsibility for the abuse by writing a letter to the victim stating:

1. I am sorry.
2. It was not your fault; it was mine.
3. It won't happen again.
4. I'm getting help now.
5. Thank you for telling.

This letter is not written until the offender is being truthful about taking responsibility for the abuse, and is often accompanied by the offender paying for counseling for the victim. This is a philosophy of reconciliation and restitution that is compatible with Christian faith.

The sex offender's therapy needs to occur within a treatment program that is knowledgeable and specialized in dealing with sex offenders. Most often, a molester will not seek help voluntarily and usually will not reveal the full extent of his problems or activities. He will often use pretended cooperation to enlist the pastor or counselor as his protector. David Peters, a Christian therapist with many years of experience in dealing with sexual abuse, writes, ". . . the average family counselor is not prepared to deal with child molesters."[25]

A case in point involved a father who was sexually abusing his 4-year-old daughter. The mother found out and went to her pastor for counseling. The pastor called the family in for counseling, where the father asked the daughter for her forgiveness. While the child's mother felt relieved that this was her husband's response, there remained many unresolved conflicts within her about the abuse. How had this ever happened? What did she do to cause it? Why did her daughter allow it to happen without telling for so long? How could she trust her husband again? Had this damaged her daughter? What had changed to

---

[24]Program for Healthy Adolescent Sexual Expression (PHASE), East Communities Family Center, Maplewood, Minn.
[25]Peters, *A Betrayal of Innocence*, 132.

prevent reoccurrence if she were not at home?

She called the pastor once again for some follow-up counseling for herself and her daughter. Her pastor informed her that it had been taken care of, that her husband had repented, and that her responsibility now was to forgive and forget because it was in the past. It was only a matter of months until the abuse resumed. This time, however, the child kept the secret.

Again, David Peters cautions pastors and Christian counselors:

> First of all, it is extremely important to the victim of sexual abuse that counselors be aware of the danger of re-molestation after sexual abuse is discovered. To accept the assurances of a molester or nonoffending parent that sexual abuse will not continue is to place the victim in danger of further abuse. It should never be assumed that the molester is able to control his sexual feelings toward the victim or the victim's siblings, no matter how socially or emotionally stable he may appear.[26]

It is essential that the offender be initially involved in individual counseling and group counseling with a peer group of sex offenders before he is permitted into a family counseling situation. He needs to be ready to take full responsibility for the abuse as well as understand the fullness of its impact on the victim and the victim's family. (See also Chapter 6.)

Barriers to Treatment Success

Several treatment issues need to be addressed in individual therapy.

Fear of Disclosure

The offender will be fearful of legal and social ramifications if the truth is known, so he will have a tendency to minimize or deny the offense. This denial will need to be confronted by not allowing him to blame others or minimize the seriousness of his behavior. When Brad Smyth, introduced at the beginning of this chapter, was confronted by his wife, he minimized his

---

[26]Ibid., 153.

responsibility for the abuse. He told his daughter that if she did "her part," and he did "his part," the abuse would not happen again. In other words, he placed much of the responsibility for preventing further abuse on his 11-year-old daughter. He then told his wife that he had "taken care of things" and instructed her not to bring it up again. When the abuse recurred, Brad's daughter assumed she had failed to do "her part" to prevent it, and she took responsibility for it, while her father remained the unrestrained perpetrator.

Dishonest Communication

The offender will need to learn basic communication skills so that he will be able to share his feelings about the abuse. Unless he is willing to be honest about his feelings—anger, fear, loneliness, sadness, loss, inadequacy—there can be little progress in therapy. Most offenders have never shared any of these feelings honestly with anyone, and will need a great deal of encouragement to see the benefit of such sharing.

Shame

Learning to overcome internalized shame is crucial to recovery. The offender will need to look in detail at his family system for shaming messages about his value as a person, at sexual messages, at issues of physical and/or sexual abuse, and at his personal, emotional, and sexual development. A sexual history will assist the offender to look at the additional impact on his life of his parents' sexual behavior, any inappropriate sexual acting out of his siblings, or possibly the previous sexual victimization of his wife by her family.

Resolving Guilt

Dealing with shame issues will help to enable the offender to begin to deal with the appropriate feelings of guilt resulting from abusing a child. Saying "I'm sorry" is not the same as asking forgiveness, just as remorse (being sorry you got caught) is not the same as repentance. True repentance is seeing his action through the eyes of his victim, and perceiving that the victim's feelings are valid. When the offender can experience the pain that he inflicted on his victim, and can take full responsibility for causing it, he is ready to confess his sin to his victim. When asking forgiveness, the offender does not merely apologize, as if the offense was something trivial, nor does he simply admit that he did something wrong. True repentance would lead the offender to tell his victim that he hurts with the pain he has caused the victim and that he realizes what he did was intolerable and inexcusable. In the context of brokenness and humility, the offender experiences true repentance and allows the victim the freedom to make an honest response to his request for forgiveness.

It may take the victim some time before he or she is able or willing to forgive the offender. Regardless of the response of the victim, the offender is held accountable before God for his actions. The offender must come before God with a broken spirit and a contrite heart and ask Him to cleanse him from his sin, and create a clean heart and a right spirit within him, as David did in Psalm 51.

After Kevin's sexual abuse of his cousin, Rhonda, Kevin entered counseling in his mid–20's for depression and shame issues. In resolving some of his personal shame from his own abuse and dysfunctional family system, and accepting his worth in God's sight, he was convicted of the guilt of his abuse of his cousin. He experienced a truly broken spirit and contrite heart over what he had done. After asking God to cleanse and forgive him, he went to his cousin, and to her mother and father, and told them about the abuse, taking full responsibility for it. In brokenness, he asked for forgiveness, and made restitution, in part, by paying for counseling for his cousin and her family. The scars from the deep pain Kevin experienced over what he had done are slowly healing, as his true repentance has borne the fruit of forgiveness from his cousin and her family.

Abandoning Power

The offender has been operating from a position of power in regard to the victim, and he will attempt to manipulate his therapy sessions to remain in a position of power. This manipulative and controlling behavior needs to be confronted not only in individual therapy, but by a group of his peers in a therapy group for sex offenders, by his victim, by his family, and by his church.

Sexual Addiction

It is imperative for the offender who is involved in an addictive cycle of sexual behavior to learn ways to cope with the everyday stress of life situations. Because he feels like a "victim" himself, inadequate to meet the demands that life makes of him, he may look to a mood-altering sexual experience as a dysfunctional coping skill. The addictive cycle, as defined by Dr. Patrick Carnes in his book *Out of the Shadows: Understanding Sexual Addiction,* progresses through a four-step cycle that intensifies with each repetition:

> 1. Preoccupation—the trance or mood wherein the addicts' minds are completely engrossed with thoughts of sex. This mental state creates an obsessive search for sexual stimulation.
> 2. Ritualization—the addicts' own special routines that lead up to the sexual behavior. The ritual intensifies the preoccupation, adding arousal and excitement.
> 3. Compulsive sexual behavior—the actual sexual act, which is the end goal of the preoccupation and ritualization. Sexual addicts are unable to control or stop this behavior.
> 4. Despair—the feelings of utter hopelessness addicts have about their behavior and their powerlessness.[27]

This despairing hopelessness that the addict feels after acting out sexually can be "medicated," masked, or numbed by beginning the preoccupation stage. As the first stage proceeds to the next, the cycle is activated once again. Dr. Carnes describes this cycle by stating, "Sexual addicts are hostages of their own preoccupation."[28] This is especially true of the fixated type of offender.

---

[27]Patrick Carnes, *Out of the Shadows: Understanding Sexual Addiction* (Minneapolis, Minn.: CompCare Publications, 1983), 9.
[28]Ibid., 9.

James 1:14–15 clearly addresses the addictive cycle:[29]

Preoccupation

*each is tempted when
by his own evil desire he
is dragged away and enticed*

Despair

*sin, when it is full grown
gives birth to death*

Ritualization

desire is conceived

Compulsive Sexual Behavior

gives birth to sin

Female Offenders

Although the majority of sex offenses are committed by men, women are also offenders. Female offenders are among the least reported cases, possibly because of their maternal caretaking role. The behavior may not be perceived as sexual or abusive because the female offender may disguise the sexual acts as normal caretaking tasks. Also, a female in a mother role is not perceived by the child victim as a sexual person. The child, therefore, does not have information that relates in any way to a sexual experience with a mother or mother-figure. If a child should protest or question the behavior, the female offender may accuse the child of having a "dirty mind." Since the female offender is often the mother or the only parent-figure giving love and care to the child, the child may continue to maintain the secret to keep the love of the parent.

The female offender usually has extreme dependency needs, may be a single parent or have an emotionally or physically absent husband, and tends to be extremely possessive and overprotective toward the child victim. Some adult offenders with such dependecy needs may use alcohol, which acts to break

---

[29]For treatment goals for the sexually addicted offender, see *Out of the Shadows: Understanding Sexual Addiction*, twelve steps to recovery, pp. 133–160.

down the barriers that would normally stop them from being sexual with children.

Susan Forward, MSW, quotes a letter from a 58-year-old woman in her book, *Betrayal of Innocence: Incest and Its Devastation:*

> My mother was a teacher and a steady churchgoer. She did the fooling around when she bathed me. I never knew there was anything unusual about her behavior until my father walked in on us and made a terrific scene. (I was twelve years old at the time—much too old to be bathed by my mother.)
>
> She never touched me after that, but the damage she had done was considerable. When I married I had a hard time enjoying sex—and still do. I was afraid to bathe my four daughters and had to force myself to do it. Even now I have trouble diapering my granddaughter.
>
> There must be others like me—grown women who still bear the marks of early abuse and have never told a soul. What a relief it has been to write this letter.[30]

Mother-Daughter Incest Offender

The mother-daughter incest offender is not primarily looking for sexual gratification, but rather nurture from physical closeness and a sense of being loved. A common history of this type of offender will reveal a childhood of physical or sexual abuse or emotional neglect and isolation. Never having received affection, she is unable to express appropriate care. The victim often remains in the abuse situation for long periods of time, sensing the extreme neediness of the mother and feeling responsible to meet those deep needs. Intense conflict usually occurs as the victim gets older, as she tries to disengage from the mother, but feels guilty for wanting to separate.

Andrea was 4 years old when her father died, leaving her mother and the three children destitute. The family moved to a small two-bedroom house where Andrea was designated to sleep with her mother. Not long after these sleeping arrangements were made, the mother began to fondle Andrea during

---

[30]Susan Forward and Craig Buck, *Betrayal of Innocence: Incest and Its Devastation* (Los Angeles: Jeremy P. Tarcher, Inc.), 117.

the night. Andrea was frozen with confusion and shame and pretended to be asleep, even though the mother sometimes took Andrea's hand and forced her to fondle her mother. No words were ever spoken at night before or after the abuse. Being extremely emotionally needy and unable to give nurture to her daughter, Andrea's mother was cold and distant during the daytime. Once, when Andrea reached up to her mother for a hug during the afternoon, her mother whirled around and slapped her face. From her warped perspective of parental discipline, the mother would lock the children in the coal bin for punishment, often for hours at a time. Because of the isolation of the family and intensely conflicting feelings which kept the children from telling, there was no intervention in the mother's abuse, and all three of her children grew up to be deeply scarred from her disturbed behavior.

Mother-Son Incest Offender

In cases of mother-son incest, the female offender places the male victim in an adult male role where he feels responsible to meet her emotional and sexual needs. The male victim "is torn between guilt, desire, love and hate. He loves his mother, yet he hates her for the guilt she has created in him by allowing the role transformation to take place."[31] Male victims can feel responsible for the abuse because there is no element of force used, and the sexual acts usually take place in a nurturing circumstance. The great travesty of this type of sexual abuse is the premature arousal and exploitation of the male victim which causes extreme guilt and shame over his participation in the sexual acts. Even when sexual actions are covert, the damage is often the same. One middle-aged man, struggling with sexually addictive behavior, shared about his tremendous conflicts arising from being a 16-year-old boy required to sleep with his mother. His mother said she couldn't "sleep comfortably" since her husband had left her unless her son slept in her bed, with his back toward her, allowing her to press her body against him.

---

[31]Ibid., 75.

Treatment Goals for Female Offenders

The limited amount of research on female offenders indicates that mother-child offenders can be extremely disturbed or even psychotic. In that case, they would only be appropriate for in-patient psychiatric hospital programs.

If the female offender is amenable to treatment, in addition to the issues listed above for male offenders, she will need to look specifically at her dependency issues and learn how to appropriately meet her emotional needs. She will also need to learn appropriate nurturing and parenting roles with her children, such as not allowing her children to sleep with her, and not bathing her preadolescent children. Learning appropriate boundaries and correcting the role-reversals in the family will be crucial in helping to develop healthy relationships with her children. (See also Family System Treatment Goals, Chapter 6.)

Section Three

Helping the Adult Victim

◇ **8** ◇

BECOMERS: An Introduction

The final section of this book is designed to equip others to facilitate the healing process for those who have been victims of childhood sexual abuse. The following chapters include the history of the development of the BECOMERS sexual abuse support group and the nine steps used in the BECOMERS recovery program, including specific material and homework to be used as a model for others who work with groups of sexual abuse victims.

BECOMERS History

Lynn Heitritter, R.N., author of *Little Ones: Protecting Your Children from Sexual Assault,* and coauthor of this book, relates the following personal account of the development of her vision as founder and director of the BECOMERS program:

Up until about 1981, I would describe myself as a very nice person who didn't talk about things that weren't "nice." Even in my experiences as a registered nurse, I had not personally known anyone who was a victim of sexual abuse. Then, in 1982, our family was introduced to sexual abuse through a young child who was being abused in her own family. That situation opened the door for us to see sexual abuse as a reality. Over a period of months, several children and adults who had been sexually abused crossed our family's path. We became a licensed foster family in order to be part of the solution to the many children who were abused.

Over the next six years, with painful realization, the hidden trauma of sexual abuse became a daily reality as I began to help those who had trusted me with their "secret." The devastation I saw in the faces of children who had been abused motivated me to be used in any way to help prevent this from happening to other children.

Out of this concern, I began to learn about sexual abuse through specialized nursing classes, reading books, and attending workshops. After the 1983 publication of my first book, *Little Ones: Protecting Your Children from Sexual Assault,* people began asking me to speak to groups of parents and in Christian schools. On each occasion where I lectured, whether in a group of 5 or 500, there were always those who approached me with their abuse history, and the struggle to recover within the context of their Christian faith.

As the awareness of the need for the Christian community to help victims of sexual abuse began to crystallize, the vision for BECOMERS was born.

During the next year, I researched the process of recovery from sexual abuse and sought counsel from many Christian therapists and other professionals, with special consultation from Jeanette Vought, coauthor of this book. This overwhelming support, professional input, and encouragement enabled me to formulate the nine steps of recovery that are now used in the program. Having pursued the vision, and after laying the groundwork, Jeanette and I combined our desires to minister to sexual abuse victims. My role, as founder, was to develop the BECOMERS program, direct it and facilitate group process with consultation from Jeanette under the administrative umbrella of New Life Family Services. In September 1984, six women entered our first BECOMERS group. Nine weeks later, with the help of a second group facilitator, Julie Woodley, we doubled our ministry and began working with sixteen women. Currently, there are BECOMERS groups across the U.S., with several new groups established internationally. One of the primary purposes of this book has been to help equip others to develop BECOMERS groups in their area because the need is far greater than our personal ability to meet it. After nearly a decade of ministry, in 1993 BECOMERS has established a new national headquarters located within the Christian Recovery Center in Minneapolis, Minnesota.

Jeanette Vought is the founder and Executive director of the Christian Recovery Center.

Jeanette says:

Because of some trauma in my own childhood experiences, I had a deep desire to help children and families. At first, this desire was realized in helping adolescents within the church. As I furthered my education, I became interested in working with female adolescents in residential treatment programs; many adolescents in treatment programs have been sexual abuse victims. Out of concern for those victims, another therapist and I began conducting sexual abuse groups.

I continued working with female sexual abuse victims for eight years. In 1981, I began working with New Life Family Services. My experiences in working with children and adolescents through foster care, in a group home, and with women in crisis pregnancies, again revealed many victims of sexual abuse. When Lynn contacted me for consultation and shared her ideas with me, I told her that I had the same perspective. God had given both of us a vision for ministry to victims of sexual abuse, and He had brought us together. My role was to give consultation to Lynn as she implemented and directed the BECOMERS program.

In 1993, God gave me a ministry vision to dedicate my time and energy solely to founding a center specializing in the areas of emotional, physical, and sexual abuse recovery. This ministry vision has resulted in establishing the Christian Recovery Center. The focus of the center will be on recovery issues for men, women, and children in both indiviudal and group settings. In addition to local ministry, the Christian Recovery Center is committed to providing consultation services, training workshops and resources, and to the development of abuse recovery groups across the country.

The BECOMERS Philosophy

BECOMERS is a support group designed to promote emotional and spiritual healing from the experience of childhood sexual abuse. BECOMERS takes its name from 1 John 3:2: "Here and now we are God's children. We don't know what we shall *become* in the future. We only know that, if reality were to break through, we should reflect His likeness, for we should see Him as He really is" (Phillips translation, italics added).

This verse speaks of the hope that it is possible to become whole and healthy even after the destruction of sexual abuse. Many of those who are victimized are unable to experience help from God in their recovery process because they have a distorted picture of God. This verse teaches that when God is seen "as He really is," one will then be able to experience His grace in healing, thus reflecting "His likeness" because the reality of His love has broken through.

The Objectives of BECOMERS

One of the most important objectives in a sexual abuse support group is to *provide a safe and accepting atmosphere* in which group members can share feelings and explore doubts related to their childhood sexual abuse. BECOMERS groups maintain strict confidentiality. BECOMERS sessions are closed to the public, allowing only group members who have completed the intake process to attend. No information about group members is shared within the group, or outside the group, unless permission is given by the individual group member for a specific purpose.

A second objective is to *provide a group support system*

which models healthy interpersonal relationships that can then provide a pattern to enhance the group member's experience of becoming whole in Christ. BECOMERS is founded on the scriptural principle of God's grace. God's grace is demonstrated through the lectures, homework, and group leaders, all of which affirm the worth of each individual in a non-shaming, accepting environment.

BECOMERS also strives to *encourage group members to actively participate with God* in the healing of their damaged emotions. BECOMERS provides lectures, homework, other materials, and group process as tools to assist group members in their recovery. Group members keep a journal and complete weekly homework. Each group member makes a commitment to attend each group session regularly, and has the option to continue or terminate at the end of each nine-week session.

A fourth purpose is to *help group members recognize and challenge negative thought patterns.* Personal sharing focuses on thought patterns and feelings resulting from sexual abuse, rather than on the detailed disclosure of explicit sexual events of the abuse. It is important to understand the source of negative thoughts, many of which came from the abuse itself.

Certain boundaries are necessary if personal sharing is to result in meaningful support. Focusing on graphic sexual acts in a support group context can occasionally foster a "competition" between group members about who suffered the greater abuse. It more often, however, inhibits group processing by those group members who feel the severity of their abuse is less valid than that of another and thus minimize the impact of their own abuse. A third stumbling block in sharing detailed sexual information is that it can become sexually stimulating to others and may re-victimize those who are listening.

BECOMERS also serves to *provide ongoing support and help* for group members. BECOMERS offers a nine-step recovery program, in which a recovery step is presented each week for nine weeks. Each recovery step focuses on different aspects of the healing process, and each nine-week session focuses on different issues of sexual abuse. Group members have the opportunity to continue in the BECOMERS program for the amount of time it takes them to complete their healing process. Members are often active in the group process for one to three years.

Finally, BECOMERS seeks to *provide support that is an adjunct to, not a replacement for, professional individual counseling.* BECOMERS groups require each group member to be in individual counseling concurrent with their participation in the BECOMERS program. A professional referral is required to begin the group entry process, which is then completed by an intake interview with a BECOMERS staff member. Each group member gives written permission to allow consultation, as needed, between the BECOMERS staff and their individual counselor.

BECOMERS Group Structure

The BECOMERS support groups meet for two hours once each week. The first half hour of group time is a teaching time where a psychologist, other professional, or BECOMERS staff person presents a topic relevant to sexual abuse. The week prior to that topic presentation, each group member has homework to complete to increase their awareness of that issue. During this teaching time, all groups meet together.

At the conclusion of the teaching, the large group breaks into pre-assigned small groups of no more than 8 group members. The purpose of the small groups is for support, application, and discussion of the homework. These small groups are in session for an hour and a half, and involve the same group members and group facilitator each week throughout the nine-week session.

At the end of the nine-week commitment, the group members may choose to continue or terminate their work with BECOMERS. Most often, each group will have changes in group members at the end of each nine-week session, but it is important to keep previous group members together, even as new members are added, to enhance the building of trust. Occasionally, some group members may need to be placed in another group. The group facilitator will need to discern when it is appropriate for a particular group member to stay in his/her group and work through difficulties in relationships with other group members or the group facilitator, or if it would be more productive for that group member to be in a different group setting.

BECOMERS Nine-Step Recovery Program

Listed below are the nine steps that are used as guidelines in the BECOMERS recovery process. The healing process, however, does not occur in such an orderly progression. Each person will need an individualized amount of time to work through specific aspects of her or his abuse. Certain aspects of the healing process may be cyclic, and personal growth in these areas may take many years. In the chapters immediately following, each step will be expanded as a model for applying these principles in the healing process.

Steps to Recovery

- Step One: I recognize that I am powerless to heal the damaged emotions resulting from my sexual abuse, and I look to God for the power to make me whole.
- Step Two: I acknowledge that God's plan for my life includes victory over the experience of sexual abuse.
- Step Three: The person who abused me is responsible for the sexual acts committed against me. I will not accept the guilt and shame resulting from those sexual acts.
- Step Four: I am looking to God and His Word to find my identity as a worthwhile and loved human being.
- Step Five: I am honestly sharing my feelings with God and with at least one other person to help me identify those areas needing cleansing and healing.
- Step Six: I am accepting responsibility for my responses to being sexually abused.
- Step Seven: I am willing to accept God's help in the decision and the process of forgiving myself and those who have offended me.
- Step Eight: I am willing to mature in my relationship with God and others.
- Step Nine: I am willing to be used by God as an instrument of healing and restoration in the lives of others.

◇ 9 ◇

Step One: Realizing Powerlessness

> Step One: I recognize that I am powerless to heal the damaged emotions resulting from my sexual abuse and I look to God for the power to make me whole.

Recognizing powerlessness, the inability to become whole through self-effort, is foundational to recovery from sexual abuse. Feeling powerless is a residual symptom of abuse, but it is often disguised by individual efforts to heal the damage, such as perfectionism, rationalization that the abuse did not have any effect, or "performance" to earn approval from others. Recovery through self-effort is perpetuated by the myth that all a person needs to recover from trauma is self-discipline and willpower.

Translated into the Christian community, such self-effort appears in many forms: performing for other Christians or for God, a "prescription" of good works involving extensive church activites, or ritualistic and compulsive Scripture reading and prayer. The sad fact about these behaviors is that they can actually become a barrier to true spiritual growth and recovery because the victims are performing for God and basing their value to God on self-effort rather than recognizing their powerlessness to heal themselves.

Accepting powerlessness lays the foundation for dependence on God. Scripture memory, prayer, and Christian fellowship are vital tools in the healing process, but the reliance on their performance as the key to healing short-circuits God's plan for experiencing the fullness of His grace through total dependence on Him. A serious concern about victims who are using their Christian performance as the basis for their personal value is that they often look so "good" that the pain they are experiencing goes unrecognized. External behavior often masks the internal conflicts of feeling that God has failed them, or that they have failed God. In either case, this unrelieved conflict can drive victimized persons into losing their faith in God, leaving the church, or remaining in the church and being dishonest about the pain that dwells within.

The process of healing begins with the restoration of personal worth, which must occur to facilitate the healing of damaged emotions. The basic issue is one of *source*. Each person needs a source which affirms that he or she is loved and accepted, worthwhile, and not alone. God is the only source with the power to confer such infinite value on each human being, and that value is based on the fullness of His love toward us, rather than on our ability to deserve it. True healing involves helping the victim to appropriate God as the only source with the power to give value, rather than giving power to others or circumstances to add value, or devalue them as a person.

A person can give away different kinds of power to others or circumstances. Victims will need to see what kinds of power they have given, or are giving away. As a child, the victim felt powerless to stop the abuse from happening or continuing, thus learning to "give" power to others. Once again, the principle of Prov. 22:6 applies. A child "trained up" to give inappropriate power and control to others, or to circumstances, may have difficulty "departing from" giving that power away inappropriately.

Victims give away physical power by allowing others to abuse them. Victimized persons need to see that there are many choices which can be made to protect their physical person. They will need to learn how to appropriate their personal power from Christ, rather than give power to others to touch them, batter them, invade their bodies, or violate their personal boundaries.

Victims often give up their emotional power as well. Because the abuse may have conditioned victims to believe that they are unable to assert themselves, or that their opinions/feelings/thoughts are invalid, they develop passive behavior. The opposite response is to react aggressively to people and circumstances. In the passive response, the power is given to others so that others are in control; thus, others become the "source" of the passive victim's sense of value. In the aggressive response, power over others is used as a means to gain self-importance by controlling others—but again, others become the "source."

Intellectual power can be regained by those victims who have been convinced that they are stupid or intellectually inadequate. God has granted each person intellectual power, and victimized persons can make choices to educate themselves about abuse, its effects, and the recovery process. Cognitive restructuring, or positive self-talk, is a helpful way to appropriate intellectual power toward healing. Scripture reading and memorization provide a basis for learning true messages about personal worth, purpose in life, and thinking patterns that promote a healthy lifestyle.

Spiritual power is the resource of divine intervention in the healing process. In 2 Cor. 12:9, Jesus states, "My grace is sufficient for you, for My power is made perfect in weakness." Because of the frequency with which this verse is quoted, often in a "quick fix" kind of answer to complicated questions, we need to take a fresh look at what Jesus is saying. The power required for healing lies in the concept of *grace.* The grace of God poured into a believer's life comes from His fullness and sufficiency. The limitless flow of grace is based on His mercy and does not depend on the worthiness of the one receiving it.

The spiritual power of grace in the context of healing sexual abuse responds to the needs of the victims to be loved unconditionally, be valued, and know they are not alone in their struggles. Christ has guaranteed His availability to meet those needs based on what He did on the cross. Not only did His death provide eternal forgiveness for the believer's sins, but made available grace to fill the inner void of feeling defective, unloved, worthless, and alone. This spiritual power is available as the believer taps into Jesus as the "source."

The battle to appropriate this truth, however, must not be underestimated. First Tim. 6:12 encourages believers to "fight the good fight of the faith." Most people are fighting the wrong fight—that is, fighting to obtain this grace by self-effort. God understands our frailties and weaknesses. As a father has compassion on his children, God says in Ps. 103:13–14, so He has compassion on those who fear Him. God knows how each of us is formed and remembers that we are dust. As dust, we are powerless to heal ourselves. The good news is that Christ has fought the fight *for* each of us, and it is finished.

The individual's responsibility is to accept the validity and sufficiency of God's provision. Because His "power is made perfect in weakness," the believer can ask God to enable him to see the weakness of deriving power from the flesh, others, or circumstances. Once these weaknesses are exposed as insufficient to heal the wounds left by the abuse, the victim needs to "fight the good fight" and ask God for the strength to stop giving power to the wrong sources and the faith to believe in the power of the One True Source. This process, on a daily basis, coupled with the resources of Steps Two through Nine, will spiritually empower the believer.

Suggested questions for homework to accompany Step One:

1. What is "power"? What does it mean to be a powerful person? What are some different kinds of power?
2. Relating to the different kinds of power in question #1, in what areas do I feel powerful?
3. What is the dictionary definition of powerlessness? What does powerlessness mean to me?
4. Describe feelings of powerlessness.
5. What is the difference between the powerlessness of being a victim of sexual abuse, and being powerless apart from God?
6. What is the difference between being a "victim" and being dependent on God?

The following art therapy technique is often helpful to assist individuals in thinking about different areas in life that might illustrate different forms of "power":

Complete your own personal "Coat of Arms" by drawing a picture or a symbol that represents the answer to each of the following questions. In space #1, draw a picture or symbol or word that corresponds to question #1 below. Complete all six questions in the same way. Bring your "Coat of Arms" to group with you.

(Feel free to change the size or shape of your "Coat of Arms" or vary it from the design below. Be sure to include all six questions in your design.)

1. What do I regard as my greatest personal achievement in life so far?
2. What do I regard as my family's greatest achievement?
3. What is the one thing people can do to make me happy?
4. What do I regard as my greatest personal failure in life so far?
5. What would I do if I had one year to live and were guaranteed success in whatever I attempted?
6. What *one thing* would I most like to be said of me?

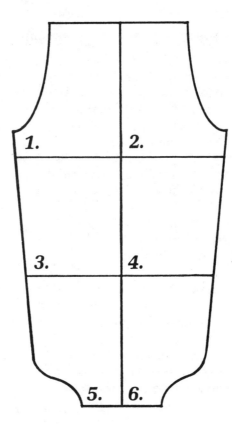

◊ **10** ◊

Step Two: Acknowledging Victory in Christ

> Step Two: I acknowledge that God's plan for my life includes victory over the experience of sexual abuse, and I look to God for the power to make me whole.

In acknowledging that God's plan includes victory over the effects of sexual abuse, the individual will need to know what "victory" means. To many people, "victory" means continually choosing correct behavior and having right attitudes about everything. Seeing such a statement in print emphasizes the impossibility of always choosing right behavior/attitudes; but in reality, many still try to live as if that were the definition of true victory. Anything less than the attainment of that perfect standard, then becomes a failure, and is thought to be "defeat."

Victory lies in experiencing one's identity in Christ, and then choosing behavior that is consistent with that identity. Victory is a process, an "identity fight," not a behavioral fight. True victory involves many learning experiences, and is usually not a one-time event, although crisis events may occur.

The diagram on the next page shows a common belief of what "victory" in Christ is.

While there is great truth in the diagram, if this cycle is the only definition of victory known to the individual, then defeat is guaranteed. And often, with the feeling of defeat, comes hopelessness.

Sherry, a 24-year-old victim with a history of three suicide attempts, visited church after church looking for the right combination of things she could do to earn God's favor, all the while

begging Him to heal her. After some intensive individual counseling, Sherry began to appropriate God's love and concluded
that if she did not have hope that God's plan for her life included
victory, then there would be no use in trying to go on.

But if God's definition of the "victorious Christian" is one
who always makes right choices, then victory will prove very
elusive to the sexual abuse victim. This is precisely the view
most sexual abuse victims have of what God expects of them in
order to have victory over the abuse.

In the BECOMERS program, when participants are given assignments to define "victory," many offer "pat answers." They
describe success/failure struggles in which they inevitably come
out the failure or they measure their value to God by their ability
to perform certain Christian behaviors. A common "pat answer"
definition of victory is that "victorious Christians" never have
struggles or defeats.

Jan, an adult victim, stated, "I *should* be able to have victory.
I wouldn't struggle if I just had enough faith." At the onset of
his BECOMERS group experience, Mark completed his home-

work by stating that there are "no victorious Christians" because God always has to keep punishing them for "wrong things they do." Mark felt that he would never be able to have victory over the abuse in his life because he could not live up to God's standards. This kind of assignment often gives both the counselor and the counselee a picture of how the counselee views victory and is often a measure of one's degree of hope for recovery.

BECOMERS presents a definition of victory that gives a much fuller picture of God's grace to the sexual abuse victim. In the diagram on the next page, we see that in following a wrong choice, the individual does sin. The person then experiences the consequences of that sin: bitterness, frustration, guilt, self-pity, self-punishment. The defeat of disobedience is very heavy; at this point, the greatest potential for victory, or devastating defeat, can occur. Recognizing that the committing of that sin reflects a choice of behavior or attitude that is not consistent with who one is in Christ, the individual can turn to the sufficiency of Christ to meet the need that the sinful behavior was insufficient to meet.

Nancy, a 35-year-old career woman, was sexually abused by her uncle during her junior high years. She was brought up in a Christian home and wanted to live her life for the Lord. She had been living with a 40-year-old man for four years. He was not interested in marriage and she felt trapped by her feelings of love for him and the knowledge that what she was doing went against her Christian value system. Many times she left him, with a sincere resolve to repent and to end the relationship, but she found herself returning to the same situation again and again. She felt defeated and convinced that there was no victory for her. She felt she had disappointed God so many times that there was no hope for her.

Through her BECOMERS group sessions, Nancy began to realize that God could accept and love her for the person she was. Her inner conflict and discomfort were caused by the choices she was making, which were not consistent with her belief in Christ. She began to view this guilt as a positive signal indicating that the "source" she was turning to for love and acceptance, her lover, was not sufficient to meet those needs. She could see the deeper issue of her sin as not merely the

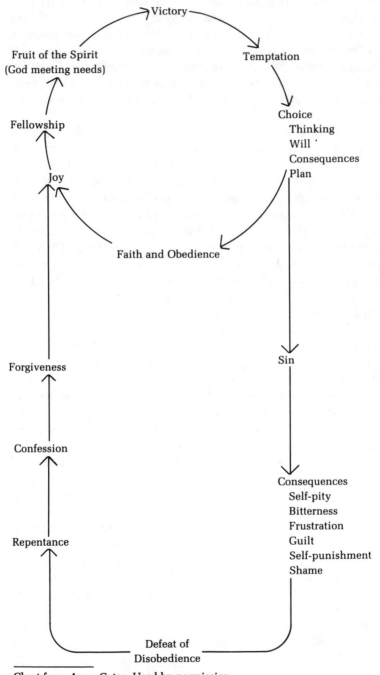

Chart from Anna Gates. Used by permission.

behavior of physical sexual acts, but one of dependency on an insufficient source.

With those who have been severely damaged by sexual abuse and have developed deeply entrenched behaviors, this may seem like "pie in the sky." Many go through the outward actions of repentance, confession, and forgiveness; but if they do not experience fellowship with God and do not experience the fruit of the Spirit, they lose hope and give up. This victory process often takes a great deal of time, and involves many aspects: changing thinking processes, accepting God's love and forgiveness, receiving help and support to maintain the hope that God's plan includes victory. Paul wrestled with similar struggles in Rom. 7:18–19: "For I have the desire to do what is good, but I cannot carry it out. For what I do is not the good I want to do; no, the evil I do not want to do—this I keep on doing." Paul felt the same kind of hopelessness and despair at times, but he reminded himself, "Thanks be to God, who gives us the victory through our Lord Jesus Christ."[1]

Suggested homework projects for Step Two:

Think about any religious training you have had.
1. Was I raised in a Christian home? If so, what did "Christian" mean in my family?
2. Was the person who abused me Christian/religious? Describe the abuser's behavior and attitudes.
3. What behaviors and attitudes did my family teach me about God? (Include verbal and nonverbal teaching.)
4. Describe a "victorious" Christian. Am *I* a "victorious" Christian?

The following is an art therapy technique that might help individuals get in touch with their view of God.

Write down thoughts as if you were writing in a diary or journal. Feel free to use any form of written expression with which you feel comfortable, i.e., poetry, prose, symbols, literal description, etc. The questions are designed to stimulate your thoughts and feelings, but are not intended to limit you to one answer per question.

---

[1] 1 Corinthians 15:57, RSV.

Think about and write down your early images of God, from the very earliest impressions/thoughts/feelings/"facts" that you can remember, all the way up to the present time.

1. What was God like?
2. How did He feel about me?
3. Where was He?
4. Where is God in this process of healing in which I am involved?
5. How do I sense His presence?
6. Draw a picture of God.

With permission, we include the following pictures of God drawn by men and women involved in our BECOMERS program. These illustrations may assist the reader to see God through the eyes of individuals who have been victimized. Not only does thinking through and drawing pictures of God reveal a great deal at the time, but if this exercise is repeated in 8–12 months, it sometimes provides an illustration of progress in this area of the healing process, as the last sequences of drawings illustrate.

etc. etc. etc.

There are no "successful" Christians. God always has to punish us for being bad. He thinks I am a loser.

ME

I feel distant and unimportant.

God

3a)

Good things
Do Do Do
Work Work Work

Bad behavior, negative
emotions, conflicts, stress,
sin.

3b)

3c)

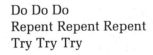

Do Do Do
Repent Repent Repent
Try Try Try

4)

God is disgusted with me;
He wishes I'd never been
born. He doesn't "see" me—
He just looks through me.
I'm angry at God and afraid
of Him. I feel abandoned
and think He is cruel.

The following series illustrate the images of God as they change during the healing process. iIt is important to note that these individuals are still in the process of becoming whole, of knowing God as He truly is.

Initial image of God:

5a)

God loves me and He sent His Son to die for me and I'd better be grateful. He is a stern, arms-crossed judge and a cold authoritarian. I never "measure up."

Change in image of God 8 months later:

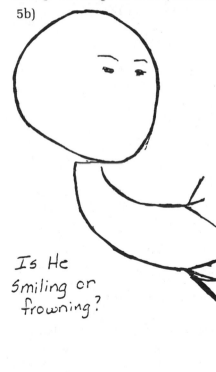

5b)

I am beginning to believe that God really does love me, but I am afraid to let go of my anger because I don't know what will happen to me if I do. Do I have to please God continually? I fail so much. . . . I still feel intimidated like I did as a child.

Is He smiling or frowning?

ME

My past
Anger
Fear Hurts

Initial image of God:

6a)

I am a failure; I never do things good enough. Deep down inside, I think I hate God.

Change in image of God 18 months later:

6b)

Right now I feel that He is pretty uncaring, that He's turned His back on me, decided to leave me alone. . . . I feel hurt when I think of God because of how I think He feels about me. I feel angry at Him for not coming through for me. But I don't hate Him. . . usually I just feel an empty apathy about Him.

(Note: The following 5 pictures illustrate a 3-year healing process.)

7a)

This is what God was doing
while I was being abused as
a child.

7b)

This is me as an adult when
I became a Christian.

I was sexually abused by an elder in the church who was supposed to be "counseling" me. This is how I saw God—He mocked people who came to Him for help and threw lightning bolts at them.

7c)

7d)

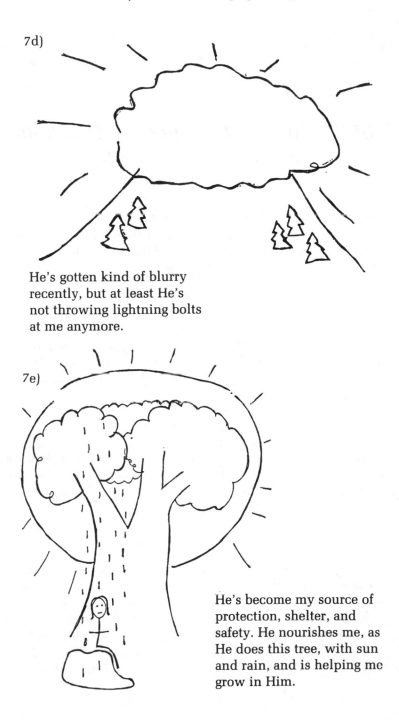

He's gotten kind of blurry
recently, but at least He's
not throwing lightning bolts
at me anymore.

7e)

He's become my source of
protection, shelter, and
safety. He nourishes me, as
He does this tree, with sun
and rain, and is helping me
grow in Him.

11

Step Three: Experiencing Freedom From Shame and Guilt

Step Three: The person who abused me is responsible for the sexual acts committed against me. I will not accept the guilt and shame resulting from those sexual acts.

Even though the offender is responsible for the sexually abusive behavior, most victims come through a childhood abuse experience with the feeling that they are to blame. A key in the recovery process is being able to distinguish between appropriate guilt and shame, so they can assume responsibility for true guilt, and let go of responsibility that is motivated by shame.

Guilt

Guilt and shame are very different. Guilt can be a status or an emotion; shame, in contrast, relates more to self-image and a view of others in relationship to self.

Guilt As a Status

Guilt can be a status that is declared judicially. A person can be declared guilty or innocent by a judge or jury regardless of the fact of their true guilt or innocence. In a spiritual dimension, prior to becoming a Christian, each person has a guilty status before God. We are declared "guilty" by being separated from God due to sin, as stated in Rom. 3:23 (TLB): "Yes, all have sinned; all fall short of God's glorious ideal." The basis of this guilty status before God is not dependent on whether one "feels" guilty or not, but rather on the sinful state of each individual.

When Adam and Eve chose to depend on themselves and lost their dependence on God, they lost true "life." God told them that on the day they ate of the forbidden fruit, they would surely die. In addition to the advent of future physical death, they experienced spiritual death. David Needham writes in his book, *Birthright: Christian, Do You Know Who You Are?*: "The Bible focuses in on what they *lost* rather than on what they acquired."[1] Adam and Eve were then aware of the piercing defectiveness of spiritual death, and of the emptiness inside which was now void of spiritual life—an emptiness reflecting the "loss" of life.

Because Adam and Eve did not take responsibility for their sin, the behavior that followed appears to be motivated by shame. Rather than approaching God in repentance, they tried to *protect* themselves from being exposed as defective, lacking, and without "life" by hiding from God, by blaming God, each other, and the serpent. They tried to *perform* to cover this defectiveness by sewing fig leaves together to hide themselves. Everyone since Adam, then, has also experienced an identity of shame.

This deficient condition of spiritual death constitutes one's guilty status before God. He has declared each of us separated from Him based on our deficiency. Yet He has made provision through Christ for that defectiveness.

God gave His law to show that we could never be "OK" by our performance. Not only could we not perform to earn His acceptance, we did not have to. His grace was a free gift.

> But God is so rich in mercy; He loved us so much that even though we were spiritually dead and doomed by our sins, He gave us back our lives again . . . all because of what Christ Jesus did. Because of His kindness you have been saved through trusting Christ. And even trusting is not of yourselves; it too is a gift from God. Salvation is not a reward for the good we have done, so none of us can take any credit for it. It is God Himself who has made us what we are and

---

[1]David C. Needham, *Birthright: Christian, Do You Know Who You Are?* (Portland, Ore.: Multnomah Press, 1979), 20.

given us new life from Christ Jesus.''[2]

Because of Christ's work on the cross, and our acceptance of that work, Rom. 8:1 says, "Therefore, there is now no condemnation for those who are in Christ Jesus, because through Christ Jesus the law of the spirit of life set me free from the law of sin and death." Once we receive life in Christ, we are in a relationship without condemnation; our guilty "status" is gone.

The chart below shows some of the basic differences between guilt and shame.

	GUILT	SHAME
SOURCE	*Conviction of Holy Spirit*	*Condemnation of the enemy, others and self*
AREA CONFRONTED	*Behavior, wrong choices*	*Identity; bad person*
MOTIVATION	*To confess*	*To internalize, keep inside*
GOAL	*Experience forgiveness*	*Experience pain*
RESULT	*Freedom, growth*	*Bondage*
OWNERSHIP	*Given to God*	*Shame "owns"/ controls me*

Guilt As a Feeling

The emotion of guilt is different from the guilty status of the unbeliever. The emotion of guilt comes from the conviction of God when we act in a way which is inconsistent with the truth in His Word. God's Holy Spirit confronts behavior and wrong choices (sin)—wrong thoughts, attitudes, or actions that are not compatible with our identity in Christ. In other words, sin is anything that gets in the way of our relationship with God.

The feeling of guilt is positive because it is a signal from God that our behavior on the outside is not matching who we

---

[2]Ephesians 2:4, 5a, 6b, 8, 9, 10a, TLB.

are on the inside. Although guilt can be a painful emotion, it is not negative unless it is ignored. Just as physical pain is a signal that something is wrong in our bodies, the purpose of guilt is to motivate us to confess our sin to God—and to others, if appropriate—and to make restitution or to take responsibility for wrong behavior. The goal of guilt is that we would experience forgiveness that leads to an experience of God's exceedingly abundant grace, freedom, and growth. "So great is his love for those who fear him, as far as the east is from the west, so far has he removed our transgressions from us."[3]

Shame

Shame differs from guilt in that it is not so much an emotion as it is a mind-set or a perception about being a defective person. Shame is feeling "bad," stupid, inadequate, incapable, a failure, worthless . . . empty. A person's self-concept is a deeply private experience. Shame gives the perception of being completely exposed and aware of being looked at (like Adam), of being visible but not ready to be visible. John Powell, in his book, *Why Am I Afraid to Tell You Who I Am?*, says, "I'm afraid to tell you who I am because if I tell you who I am, you may not like who I am, and it is all that I have."[4]

Shame usually originates from specific beliefs we are taught about ourselves by family members or other significant people. Shame is perpetuated by treating ourselves the way we were treated by others and giving ourselves the same "messages" we were given by others. Sometimes Satan launches attacks of condemnation upon us in an attempt to convince us that our shame messages are truthful. Sometimes this condemnation affects those who feel that they are not forgiven even after they have repented in response to feelings of guilt. This cycle can be detected in individuals who have taken appropriate steps to ask forgiveness and make necessary restitution, yet still feel that they are not forgiven. In such a case, the person is no longer struggling with guilt, but with a sense of shame.

Shame attacks the identity of a person; guilt involves a con-

---

[3]Psalm 103:11b–12.
[4]John Powell, *Why Am I Afraid to Tell You Who I Am?* (Valencia, Calif.: Tabor Publishing, 1969), 21. Used by permission.

frontation of sinful behaviors. While guilt "messages" state "I made a bad choice," shame messages say "I am a bad person." Shame motivates victims to internalize the pain of feeling defective; the result is either to protect themselves or to perform. The end result is bondage, not the freedom that is found in forgiveness after confessing true guilt.

The tragedy of shame is that, unlike the guilt, which is confessed to God and removed, the shame actually "owns" people and holds them in bondage. The bondage of shame reminds us of the figure of Lazarus as he was called forth from the tomb by Christ. He was very much alive, and yet bound up with heavy grave clothes. Christ's instructions to Lazarus' friends were to "unbind him." Such is the work of the Holy Spirit, who uses God's truth and caring members of the body of Christ to help unbind the heavy layers of shame.

Signs and Signals of Shame

Unlike Lazarus, whose bondage was quite visible, identifying a person in bondage to shame is not always easy. The following warning signals may help to evaluate when a person is experiencing shame:

1. An "I am bad/defective/don't measure up" feeling.
2. Wanting to hide or disappear from the presence of others.
3. Trying to "prove" to God or others that I am important or special, i.e., by overachievement, by needing to be "right," by being the best at everything.
4. Punishing myself with physical punishments: cutting self, burning self with cigarettes, being accident prone.
5. Punishing myself with emotional punishments: setting myself up to be hurt or rejected by others, negative or destructive self-talk.
6. Often feeling "defensive" when criticized, whether the criticism is constructive or destructive.
7. Feeling fearful when someone wants to establish a close and caring relationship.
8. A drooping body posture—slouching shoulders, hanging of the head, avoiding eye contact.
9. "Acting out" behaviors: drugs, alcohol, arson, cruelty to others or to animals, stealing, prostitution, suicide attempts, eating disorders, compulsive behaviors.

Sources of Shame

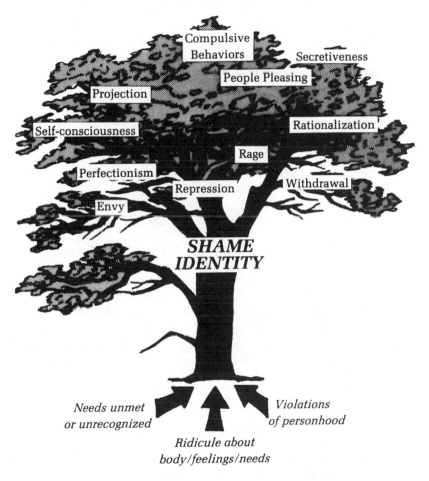

The Faces of Shame

I feel
    like a tree who has been defoliated,
      a slender birch
      who has been stripped
        of her bark.
My trunk has become a dart board
    for the archer.
Inscribed on my spine
    is the word SHAME.
My limbs have been twisted,
    they hang by my side.
The sap has been drained
    from my punctured veins.
My larynx is ruined.
    I cannot scream.
The birds of the air
    are awed by their vision.
The deer cannot watch.
The squirrels bury their heads.
Even the rodents run from the sight.
The sun looks away
    and my blackness remains.

—Jane Ault[5]

Many faces can hide the inner feelings of shame. Some of the more frequent "faces" encountered in working with victims of sexual abuse are:

1. They are tired—physically, emotionally, and spiritually exhausted. They are tired of trying to please others, of trying to please God, and often just tired of living.

2. They have a shame-based identity, most always feeling that something is wrong with them or that they are "less than" others. This identity produces a "shame filter" that colors every aspect of life. This "shame filter" hears shame messages, even when they are not intended. This "shame filter" governs their responses to life circumstances, such as finding it very difficult to admit mistakes and always having to be "right."

---

[5]Jane Ault, 1989. Used by permission.

3. They feel that their value comes from what they do or don't do, what they have or don't have. This faulty perception that approval depends on performance makes it very difficult for them to believe they can be loved, adequate, and accepted for free. They will tend to think they must earn or repay any acceptance they receive from God or others. They find it very hard to accept gifts, whether it is the free gift of salvation from God or material gifts, compliments, or other rewards from others.

4. They are unaware of personal needs or how to get those needs met. Because of not knowing what "normal" needs are and how they can be appropriately met, the "norm" for them might be feeling that they should not even HAVE needs, or that others are totally responsible for meeting their needs.

5. They usually feel over-responsible for things that happen. They develop "radar" that looks for signals in situations around them to see what they did to "cause" the circumstance to happen. Their "radar" also tunes in to find out what they need to "do" to be accepted. Their "radar" is often extremely accurate in picking up dysfunctional problems; but because of their shame "filter," they do not trust their "radar" and usually end up feeling that *they* are the problem, instead of the problem being the problem.

6. They tend to be "martyrs," feeling helpless and incapable, perpetuating their role as "victim," and are often victimized by others.

7. They do not often speak directly or straightforwardly, especially about their feelings.

8. They feel as if they don't "belong," desperately wanting intimacy but being afraid of others and pushing them away.

9. They cannot have guilt-free fun, because they feel they don't deserve to take time for themselves; if they are not producing something, they have no value.

10. They often have "idols" as their source of life—pleasing others, children, spouse, money, sex, ministry, food. When the seeking of life from these idols continues in the face of negative consequences, an addiction occurs.

11. They are "survivors" of their sexual abuse, but they tend to stay in relationships where they can use those same "survival

skills" rather than taking the risk to learn new skills to get out of negative situations.

12. They have a very hard time trusting God or people.[6]

Recovery From Shame

One of the first starting points in recovery from shame is breaking silence about the "secrets" surrounding the abuse. Sharing those secrets needs to take place in a safe and caring environment and with those who are trustworthy. This sharing will help the individual to identify shaming messages that they received, perhaps from many sources, in addition to the abuse. Growth and freedom from shame will occur as the victim talks about experiences about which she or he feels shame.

Another step in the recovery process is for the victim to see the importance of getting support from others—a therapist, a pastor, a support group or a combination of these resources. It is difficult for sexual abuse victims to ask for support because they feel unworthy of receiving help. A concrete way to confront shame is to receive new feedback about oneself from supportive sources. This feedback will help the victim to confront the original sources of shame with the true messages about their abuse and their family system, as well as messages about who they are in Christ. This is a practical application of Rom. 12:2, which encourages transformation by the renewing of the mind.

Such renewing of the mind, along with the expression of true feelings, will begin to rebuild damaged self-esteem. This rebuilding process will enable victims to experience some compassion for the abused children they once were, so that they will not continue to treat themselves in the manner in which they were treated by others.

Developing an awareness of defense mechanisms (see Step Six) that have accumulated for survival or protection is another key in recovering from shame. Defense mechanisms have usually evolved from many years of trying to cope with the effects of the abuse, and in that regard may seem to have served a useful purpose. In the process of recovery, the grip of these defense mechanisms can be released as the victim is strengthened

---

[6]Jeff VanVonderen, *Tired of Trying to Measure Up* (Minneapolis, Minn.: Bethany House Publishers, 1989).

enough to let go of the protection they provide. It is important for victims to learn more appropriate defense mechanisms to protect their personal boundaries or when they are in unsafe environments.

Victims will need to examine their present relationships and behaviors to see if they are healthy or shame-producing. Sometimes it is discovered that present relationships feel like the web of childhood, reenacted in adult situations. The development of healthy adult relationships provides freedom, support, affirmation, and openness in communication.

Religious Solutions to Shame
vs.
God's Solution to Shame

Religious solutions to shame often put people under the "law" by requiring ritualistic performance of certain Christian behaviors. Religious systems tend to define "victory" as perfect external behavior rather than focusing on the internal victory of identity in Christ. This performance mentality tends to push people into a cycle of trying hard to self-improve and then subsequently giving up, because trying hard is not the solution to shame. This solution generates very, very tired people.

God's solution to shame focuses on the inner resources provided by daily dependence on Him. The struggle against shame is an identity issue rather than a behavioral issue—appropriating value and peace from God on the inside, not just exhibiting "good" behavior on the outside. Change in outside behavior results from learning to act in a way that is consistent with what is true on the inside. God's commitment to restoration for the tired and weary person is found in Matt. 11:28, 29: "Come to me all you who are weary and burdened and I will give you rest. Take my yoke upon you and learn from me, for I am gentle and humble in heart, and you will find rest for your souls. For my yoke is easy and my burden is light." "Weary and burdened" in this verse refers to striving and carrying a load that grinds one to powder, which is exactly the way the shame of the sexual abuse victim feels. But God, who is our Source, promises to provide rest.[7]

---

[7]Adapted from: Jeff VanVonderen, *Tired of Trying to Measure Up* (Minneapolis, Minn.: Bethany House Publishers, 1989).

Homework for shame recovery

The following homework projects, developed for use in the BECOMERS program, can be used over a period of several weeks.

Shame homework project 1

It is essential to identify where the "messages" came from that convince us that we are "shameful" and "bad." Once those "messages" are exposed and brought into the light of what is true about us as individuals, we have the risky but freeing opportunity to make some choices about how we view ourselves.

Look through the following indicators of a shame-based family system. Which ones were (or are) present in the family in which you were raised? You can describe your birth home, an adoptive home, a foster home or any combination of living situations that have left "messages" with you.

1. Was I shamed in front of others for my behavior? If so, write about a specific time.

2. Was I belittled/ridiculed? About what?

3. Was I constantly compared to another child? Who?

4. Was I humiliated in front of others? Who did that to me?

5. Did I somehow feel that I was a "disappointment" to my parents? In what way?

6. Was I expected to be "perfect"? Did I ever feel as if I were "good enough"?

7. Did it seem it was my responsibility to make sure no one's feelings were hurt and that there was no conflict?

8. Did either of my parents communicate to me (either with words or by their attitude) that they were "helpless" to do anything about any problems in the family? Have I sometimes found myself feeling "trapped" with my circumstances, feeling as if things will never change for me?

9. Was there physical violence in my family? Who physically abused me? Write about a specific incident.

10. Was there an attitude of seduction with sexual comments that were made to me by someone in my family? Was anyone in my family involved in any form of pornography—magazines (either "soft" or "hard core" pornography), movies, photo-

graphing others? Was anyone in my family involved in same-sex relationships?

11. Were there addictions in my family, such as drugs, alcohol, sexual addictions, overeating, compulsive gambling, compulsive overspending, workaholism?

12. What were relationships like within my family?

    a. Enmeshed: all mixed up, no boundaries, everyone over-involved with each other, no privacy. Did the things I said and did seem to be important to how my parents felt about/toward themselves and me?

    b. Isolated: everyone keeping to themselves, stuffing feelings, no communication.

    c. Overcontrolling: rigid rules, "legalistic."

    d. Chaotic: no one seeming to be in control, unsupervised freedom, lack of concern about me, neglect (lacking either physical or emotional nurture, or both).

    e. Perfectionistic: an "all-or-nothing" kind of feeling in my family—"either you do what I want or you don't love me . . ." or "everything is either wonderful or terrible . . ." with any situation that was not considered perfect being considered terrible.

13. Did I feel that I always had to "look good" or "do the right thing" so that it would look good to others?

14. In my family, was someone always to blame whenever anything didn't go as planned? Was I punished when I made mistakes?

15. How does my family define success? Am I a success?

16. When there was trouble in my family or some kind of conflict, did my family deny it by ignoring it?

After you have answered these questions, think over what you've written for a day or two. Then finish up your work by answering the following: Summing up all your thoughts above, write out 3 or 4 "messages" you have believed about yourself that are a direct result of what others have communicated to you about you.

Shame homework project 2

Often it is difficult for a sexual abuse victim to get in touch with shame experienced in childhood, especially if those feelings have been repressed for a long time. The following homework has been effective in helping to release these feelings of shame.

Bring a photo of yourself as a child to your group as part of your homework.

Attach photo here:

Looking at the child in the photo, complete the following statements:

This child was sexually abused by . . .

This child was sexually abused because . . .

This child needed . . .

This child felt . . .

This child believed that . . .

This child decided to . . .

If I were to adopt this child, I would . . .

because . . .

Considering some of the negative "messages" this child received, write about some differences between shame messages and guilt messages.

Where does guilt come from?

Where does shame come from?

How would the child in this photo know the difference?

How does shame affect the child in this photo in response to self? To others?

How does shame affect this child's use of an inner source of adequacy/power/control, or, letting others control this child?

Contrast these thoughts about yourself as a child with the thoughts and responses you now have as an adult.

How does shame affect my responses to myself and to others, now that I am an adult?

How does shame affect my use of power/control in my adult life? Am I allowing others to exercise power/control over me or to "use" me?

These questions can be a very powerful tool to help the victim identify true inner shame. Some have answered these questions in profound ways:

"This child was sexually abused because

. . . she was born.

. . . she had sick parents who took out their misery on her and got away with it because no one cared.

. . . of his need to be nurtured from a father figure.

. . . because she developed too soon.

. . . because she didn't say no.

. . . because she was there, and she was small."

"This child needed . . .

. . . to be stillborn.

. . . to be born to other parents.

. . . to be taken out of the home.

. . . someone to listen to her.

. . . to have someone care about him and help him.

. . . love and attention from her dad.

. . . she really needed her mom."

"This child felt . . .

. . . powerless.

. . . momentary satisfaction and acceptance from someone he thought really cared.

. . . feelings of guilt for allowing the abuse to happen.

. . . that she deserved her treatment because she wasn't worthy of anything better.
. . . that life will never change.
. . . confused, abandoned, rejected, alone."

"This child believed . . .
. . . that something was wrong with her, that she was bad.
. . . that sexual feelings were bad and were to be kept secret.
. . . it was OK to be abused as long as it made Dad happy.
. . . that it was an acceptable way to show love.
. . . that she was unloved, despised and worthy of ugly, abusive treatment.
. . . that if she told anyone, she would get in a lot of trouble."

"This child decided . . .
. . . to withdraw and put up a front to be whatever those around her wanted her to be.
. . . to play along and hide what she was really feeling.
. . . that no one could be trusted and everyone was out to hurt her.
. . . to just be quiet and forget about it."

"If I were to adopt this child, I would . . .
. . . show the child more love in a nurturing, nonsexual way, because otherwise the child will look for acceptance in a sexual way.
. . . help him to feel loved and safe about talking about his feelings because he is a special person and very gifted.
. . . not do it because she has wounds and scars that are too deep to heal. The best I could do is leave her alone and not hurt her anymore.
. . . hold her as long as she wanted to be held and give her lots of hugs."

These comments reflect some of the depth of the pain of an abused child. Because of the intensity of the pain, it is sometimes easier to begin to get in touch with these feelings by first looking at them in a somewhat detached way, such as using a childhood photo, and then applying those insights to present adult life.

Shame homework project 3

In addition to understanding the difference between shame and guilt, and getting in touch with shame messages, the victim will need to separate areas of responsibility for the abuse. The following homework will help to assess how much responsibility the victim is carrying for the abuse.

1. What have I told myself that I am responsible for concerning my abuse?

2. What do I think are the responsibilities of the offender/offenders concerning my abuse?

3. In God's sight, what am I responsible for?

4. In God's sight, what is the responsibility of the offender?

5. How have I taken responsibility for the abuse, or parts of the abuse, that are not my responsibility?

6. What hinders me from "letting go" of being responsible for the abuse?

The issue of who is responsible for the abuse is critical in recovery. These kinds of questions reveal many insights as the victim works through them. Some discovered that they felt responsible for the abuse because they were quiet and didn't resist; because there were some "good feelings" associated with the abuse, they were told they were responsible for it, or because God had "predestined" them to be abused. There can be many barriers to letting go of taking responsibility for the abuse. Some have written that they struggle with thinking they are "garbage," that something must be "wrong" with them, believing that others must be right or more important, feeling that nothing can change and feeling that God does not care.

A Note on Sexual Shame

Sexual shame is a residual effect of sexual abuse and sexual messages from the family system. These difficult issues must be faced in the light of God's truth and His atmosphere of love. Questions may arise about exposing individuals to this kind of introspection. However, these buried areas of sexual shame are actually "buried alive." If they are not exposed to the Light for cleansing and healing, they will continue to control the inner person, and may be the instrument of abuse to self and others; ultimately, they may hinder victims from fullness in their relationship with God.

Shame homework project 4

Identifying Sexual Shame

Childhood Messages	Me	Spouse/Other
1. What were early "messages" in your family about your body?		
2. What were your parents' attitudes about nudity/ modesty?		
3. What did you learn in your family—who told you and how did you feel —about pregnancy?		
4. —about birth?		

(continued)

Identifying Sexual Shame (cont.)

Childhood Messages	Me	Spouse/Other
5. —about intercourse?		
6. —about masturbation?		
7. —about homosexuality?		
8. —about venereal disease?		

(continued)

Identifying Sexual Shame (cont.)

Sexual Abuse History	Me	Spouse/Other
1. Sexual activity with older person/people: —your age —age of other person/s —what kind of activity —looking —genital touching —vaginal penetration —oral/genital contact —anal contact —other		
2. Did you observe parents or others having intercourse? —hearing them —seeing them Describe feelings.		

(continued)

Identifying Sexual Shame (cont.)

Adolescent/Adult Experiences	Me	Spouse/Other
1. Masturbation —age when began —ever punished? —frequency —method (self/others) —accompanying fantasies —marriage partner's knowledge of		
2. Necking/"Making out" —age when began —frequency —number of partners —types of activity		
3. Intercourse —frequency —numbers of partners —sex of partner (opposite/same) —kinds of partners (spouse/fiancee/lover/friend/prostitute/unselective) —feelings about premarital intercourse		
4. Use of pornography? —frequency —type (x-rated movies/video/adult bookstore)		

(continued)

Identifying Sexual Shame (cont.)

Feelings About Masculinity	(If Male)	
	Me	*Spouse/Other (about me)*
1. Do you feel masculine? 　—popular? 　—sexually adequate? 　—any feelings about being a "sissy"? 　—feel accepted by peers?		
2. What are your feelings about 　—body size (height/ weight) 　—appearance (handsomeness/ virility) 　—voice 　—hair distribution 　—genitals (size, ability to respond sexually)		

(continued)

Identifying Sexual Shame (cont.)

Feelings About Femininity	*(If Female)*	
	Me	*Spouse/Other (about me)*
1. Do you feel feminine? —popular? —sexually adequate? —ever considered a "tomboy"? —feel accepted by peers?		
2. What are your feelings about —body size (height/ weight) —appearance (beauty) —breast size, hips, genitals		

(continued)

Identifying Sexual Shame (cont.)

Feeling About	Me	Spouse/Other
1. Dating/Engagement —sexual activity —kissing, French kissing —making out —intercourse —number of individuals —feelings		
2. Marriage —premarital sex? —describe sexual relationship of honeymoon (pleasant/ unpleasant) —wife aroused/ husband aroused? —was spouse considerate? —any complications (impotence, frigidity, pain) —sex in marriage —your general satisfaction or dissatisfaction sexually —what are your thoughts about the general satisfaction or dissatisfaction of your spouse? —extramarital sex?		

Write about other messages you received about sexuality:

Messages may be spoken, or unspoken; sometimes they may be identified as "instinctive feelings", such as, "Sex is dirty." "Be sure to save it for the one you love." "*Nice* girls don't enjoy sex." or "Real men take sex any way they can get it."

When dealing with sexual issues, a careful balance must be maintained. As important as it is for the victim to have permission to tell the "secrets," it is equally important for others not to be victimized by the details of the sexual acts in which the victim has been involved. The BECOMERS perspective encourages group members to fully share their thoughts and feelings about their abuse. Graphic physical details and word-picture descriptions, however, can be a stumbling block or actually victimize or re-victimize those who are listening. In the cases where victims are struggling with sexual fantasies, explicit graphic sharing will feed the fantasy and impede progress. An accompanying issue in the group process is the comparison that occurs after the graphic disclosure of physical sexual events within the group. This may cause some to try to overstate their abuse incidents to compete with another's story. More commonly, it may cause those who have experienced fewer incidents or abuse that appears to be of lesser degree to minimize the pain and effects of their own abuse.

12

Step Four: Discovering Self-Identity

> Step Four: I am looking to God and His Word to find my identity as a worthwhile and loved human being.

All people struggle at times with feelings of inadequacy and self-worth. But those who have been sexually victimized have an even greater struggle to face.

In her book *Secret Shame: I Am a Victim of Incest,* Martha Janssen shares her struggle in finding her identity as a valuable person.

Thirteen

Textbooks say that thirteen
is the age when one
wrestles with identity.
Am I weak or strong
    loved or rejected
    female or male
    capable or inept?
Who am I? the child-adult wonders.
I wondered too.
I stood before the screen door
looking at the countryside
from Grandpa's house in summer.
I was blank inside
    lonely
    bored
    wondering.
I was struggling
    wrestling
not just with identity

but with what you said about me
by what you did.
I was weak—
you always won.
I was rejected—
you went away angry.
I was female—
and hated it.
I was not capable
because I could not change my life.
Young, tender, frightened
I was a textbook case of the struggle
and doomed to lose.
A blank empty life
looking out the screen door.[1]

Developmental stages in the establishment of an individual's personal identity begin in infancy and build upon one another. According to developmental psychologist Erik Erikson,[2] trust is a major building block for a healthy identity. Learning to trust begins in infancy and is the foundation for the toddler to learn about autonomy (independence) versus shame (inadequacy). This stage of learning independence is expressed through a natural curiosity, exploration and the famous "no" of 2-year-olds. If parents respond to this developmental task in a healthy way by setting appropriate boundaries and yet not shaming the child, the child will progress toward a healthy identity formation.

During the elementary school years, a child learns from the responses of others around him to take initiative and try new things. These attempts at learning to master the environment and learn new skills will be met by responses from others. If those responses are supportive, the child will gain another foundational block upon which his identity will be built.

In adolescence, children are searching for the answers to who they are. As her poem demonstrates, Janssen, as an adolescent, had a severely damaged identity. Early sexual abuse

---

[1]Martha Janssen, *Secret Shame: I Am a Victim of Incest* (Minneapolis: Augsburg Fortress, 1991). Reprinted by permission.
[2]Norman A. Sprinthall and W. Andrew Collins, *Adolescent Psychology: A Developmental View* (New York: Random House, 1984), 33.

violates trust, creates a "victim" mind-set instead of a healthy independence, and leaves shame as the source of self-identity. Shame blocks taking initiative, taking risks in personal growth and achievement, and leaves the abused child with a profound sense of inferiority.

A Victim Identity

A damaged identity can produce many unhealthy attitudes. An attitude of hopelessness convinces us that we are "frozen" in the pain of present circumstances, that things have never been good and that they will never get any better. It seems to such a person that pain is unending and irreversible. Many victims have such a mind-set of hopelessness.

Helplessness stems from a feeling that we have no control over what happens in our lives. It seems that our fate depends on other people's evaluations of us, or luck, or factors outside our control. Even God isn't there—or, if He is there, He has no control. Revictimization is a common occurrence for the person whose attitude is one of helplessness.

Self-condemnation is a mind-set of viewing ourselves as nothing. We are unable to have positive regard for ourselves, let alone love ourselves. We attach negative labels to ourselves: "I am unlovable," "I am ugly," "I am bad," "I am lazy." These labels can easily become self-fulfilling prophecies. Perfectionism compounds the self-defeat because goals and standards are unattainable. Trying to develop motivation with moralistic "shoulds" and "oughts" leads to resentment, tension, and false guilt. Frustration runs high when a person has unrealistic goals and yet tries to accomplish those goals easily and quickly. The effort that is required to make changes seems too great and the rewards not worth struggling for. The victim who has an attitude of self-condemnation will continually feel defeated.

Victims can become paralyzed by a fear of failure, so overwhelmed that they refuse to try to change. The victim blows a simple task out of proportion until it becomes impossible to achieve, or tries to tackle a task without breaking it down into manageable steps. Being consumed about many little things that need to be done is another way to avoid the task at hand. Because the healing process seems overwhelming to many victims, some don't ever try to recover. Others try but give up, and still others distract themselves from their need to get help.

Due to a lack of confidence, some may fear success even more than failure. Success may be viewed as a danger because the victim feels it will heighten people's expectations. The underlying fear of being discovered as a failure, with its subsequent rejection and pain, may make success seem like an undesirable risk. A victim with this attitude will tend to avoid commitment or involvement.

These attitudes are components of a damaged identity. The sexual abuse victim needs help to make the transition from a damaged identity to a healthy Christ-centered identity; from an identity of inadequacy to one of competency and fulfillment; from an identity of hopelessness and helplessness to one of hope and capability; from an identity that condemns and hates self to one that loves self.

Loving Ourselves

The phrase "loving ourselves" may trigger thoughts of vanity or pride or humanistic self centeredness. While these types of self-love are inconsistent with Scripture, it is possible to love ourselves in a healthy way that honors God and makes us more useful in His service. In Mark 12:28, a scribe came to Jesus and asked Him which commandment was most important. In verses 30 and 31, Jesus replied, "Love the Lord your God with all your heart and with all your soul and with all your mind and with all your strength. The second is this: Love your neighbor *as yourself*. There is no commandment greater than these" (NIV, italics ours).

Dr. Paul Meier, in his book *Christian Child-Rearing and Personality Development,* writes: "A person who has a negative attitude toward himself will also be quite critical of others. A person who doesn't love himself in a healthy way will find it impossible to develop genuine love relationships with others. Two of the most important concepts I learned from my psychiatric training, both of which agree totally with Scripture, are: (1) You cannot truly love others until you learn to love yourself in a healthy way. (2) Lack of self-worth is the basis of most psychological problems."[3]

Often the church has resisted any positive reference to self-love. Tim Stafford, writing in *Do You Sometimes Feel Like a Nobody?*, explains some of this religious resistance to self-love.

> But some . . . I believe oversimplify the Bible and sometimes hurt people with emotional problems. Without wanting to badmouth them, I will refer to people who believe this as the "Nothings" because they say, repeatedly, "I am nothing; Christ is everything." . . . They emphasize that all pride is bad. I think all Christians would agree that there is a kind of pride that is deadly—the pride that says to God "I am self-sufficient. I don't need you. I'll make it on my own." But Nothings believe in extinguishing all pride—pride in a good job, pride in an act of kindness, pride in an attractive, healthy body. They think it detracts from loving God. They quote Paul: "If I am going to boast, let me boast in the Lord."
>
> Also, Nothings believe that all our problems were destroyed when Jesus died on the cross, and that we are meant to have the full results of that immediately. Thus all problems are religious problems; a person is depressed or discouraged or sick only because he hasn't "yielded" to God, or "put God on the throne of his life. . . ."
>
> A Nothing philosophy can work, especially for people blessed with a strong ego and a stable personality. Since these people already tend to think highly of themselves, the Nothing philosophy keeps their feet on the ground. Others are damaged by such a philosophy, as in the case of Rob, a new Christian with problems. But for Rob, who tends to think poorly of himself, it (Nothing philosophy) didn't seem to help at all. While in theory Rob was giving more glory to God by "living in faith," in practice he was giving God a bad reputation. Rob was full of religious talk but almost empty of long-term religious results. It was plain to nearly everyone that he had not left his problems behind, and that he needed to deal with them.[4]

Rob has identity problems similar to those experienced by

---

[3]Paul D. Meier, *Christian Child-Rearing and Personality Development* (Grand Rapids: Baker Book House, 1984), 25–26.

[4]Tim Stafford, *Do You Sometimes Feel Like a Nobody?* (Grand Rapids: Zondervan Publishing, 1980).

sexual abuse victims. Many victimized persons who are Christians try to follow the same philosophy as Rob—and obtain the same results. Christians need to remember that God said men and women were created in His image and that they were created "very good" (Gen. 1:27). Even though we are not worthy of God's love, we are nevertheless so worthwhile to Him that He sent His Son to die for us (John 3:16). Even though mankind has fallen into sin and been disobedient for thousands of years, R.C. Sproul writes: "Man's dignity rests in God who assigns an inestimable worth to every person. Man's origin is not an accident but a profoundly intelligent act by One who has eternal value, by One who stamps His own image on each person. God creates men and moves heaven and earth to redeem them when they fall. Our origin is in creation and our destiny is for redemption. Between these points every human heartbeat has value."[5]

A Christ-Centered Identity

To have a healthy self-identity as a Christian, it is helpful to be able to view ourselves as made in God's image. God is a personal being, and people are created as personal beings. God thinks rationally, and those created in His image also have the capacity to think rationally. God makes volitional choices and has endowed individuals with the ability to make choices. Scripture indicates that God expresses emotions, and He has created people with the same potential.

As a sexual abuse victim begins to exchange the victim identity for a healthy Christ-centered identity, the following changes, adapted from Dr. Lawrence J. Crabb, Jr., will be "signposts" on the road to recovery.

Personal Health

One of the signs that we are created in God's image is our capacity for personal relationships. We are created as personal beings needing relationships, significance, and security. If we are healthy Christians and have a full personal realization of

[5]R.C. Sproul, *In Search of Dignity* (Ventura, Calif.: Regal Books, 1983), 94.

ourselves as being secure and significant in Christ, then we will:
- be willing to fail;
- remain objective, nondefensive, and compassionate when others disapprove of us, put us down, disagree with us;
- be open to looking at faults;
- remain steadfast in the midst of a crisis, and determined to live for the Lord;
- enjoy and be greatly strengthened by encouragement and positive results from efforts, but will be willing to serve Christ if encouragement does not come and efforts fail.

Rational Health

A rationally healthy Christian is not obsessed with *why* things happen as they do because God is sovereign and loving and works according to His plans. A rationally healthy Christian:
- asks the Lord to guide him/her in what to do;
- fills his/her mind with things that promote knowledge of Christ;
- sets his/her goal to please God and minister to others out of the fullness of God within.

Volitional Health

A volitionally healthy Christian is one who can choose to do whatever should be done in any given situation because Christ continually gives the strength. A volitionally healthy Christian:
- can say, "I feel this way but . . . I know I am secure and significant in Christ. Knowing that, what would I then do?"
- can say, "If I were not dealing with my old thought patterns and my old feelings, what would then be my response?"
- is able to choose freely.

Emotional Health

Emotional health for the Christian is the courage to acknowledge and accept whatever emotions exist at a given moment. Biblical counseling should never deal with the "should" without first realistically facing and acknowledging emotions. An emotionally healthy Christian will:

- acknowledge to God and to himself how he feels;
- choose to express that feeling only if it will promote God's purpose;
- let himself literally and subjectively feel the emotion that is there, trusting God for His power to continue right choices, even as he feels acute pain;
- realize that love, joy, peace, patience, kindness, goodness, faithfulness, gentleness, and self-control are spiritual attributes, not emotions;
- realize that feelings in themselves are automatic and morally neutral. The choice of how a Christian responds to emotions makes them good or bad.[6]

One of the most difficult struggles of sexual abuse victims is to believe that they are worthwhile and loved. Tim Stafford writes: "I never knew anyone who changed his self image simply by sitting and contemplating God's love for him."[7] Jesus says in Matt. 7:7, "Ask and it will be given to you; seek and you will find; knock and the door will be opened to you."

Changing one's identity is a process in which the victim will need to participate actively. The individual needs to "seek" to make changes, and "knock" on many doors to find a supportive environment in which to experience change.

Homework Questions

1. How do I define self-identity?
2. What terms do I use to define or describe myself?
3. If I had the power to do so, what would I like to change about myself?
4. What do I like about myself?
5. Who has ever made me feel loved and worthwhile? How have they done that?
6. Who has ever made me feel defective, inadequate, as if I don't "measure up"?
7. What things do I do (my performance) in order to get people

---

[6]Material adapted from Dr. Lawrence Crabb, Jr., by Anna Gates.
[7]Stafford, *Do You Sometimes Feel Like a Nobody?*, 97.

to see me as a "somebody"—a person of value of worth?

8. What things don't I do (my protection) so that people will not find out how I feel about myself on the inside?

9. How effectively has my "performance" or my "protection" worked in developing a healthy self-identity?

10. After reading Ephesians, chapters 1–3:

    a. Who does God say that I am?

    b. Who do I say that I am?

As a practical tool to assist you in picturing the process of "renewing your mind" by replacing the false image of yourself with the true image from God's Word, do the following:

> Picture a large, clear vase about half full of dark, murky water. Your job is to fill the vase with clean, fresh water until it no longer appears cloudy and dirty, and you have only an eyedropper to do it with. After the first few drops, you can see no significant change. Don't give up! Little by little, drop by drop, continue to add the clean water. Eventually you will begin to see a difference. The water inside the vase is a little less dingy. The more water you add, the cleaner the water becomes. While there will be residual effects, you have made significant improvements. This is much like the process we use as victims of incest and other wounds that make our self-image murky. As we incorporate the clear truth of God's Word, the false notions of the enemy that have corrupted our vessel begin to disseminate.[8]

---

[8]Jan Frank, *A Door of Hope* (San Bernardino, Calif.: Here's Life Publishers, 1987), 161.

Step Five: Sharing Feelings

> Step Five: I am honestly sharing my feelings with God and with at least one other person to help me identify those areas needing cleansing and healing.

God has created each individual with the capacity to experience a variety of feelings: happiness and sadness, anger and peacefulness, fear and contentment. Life circumstances, and a person's perception of those life events, evoke a myriad of feelings each day. Part of being fully human is being able to experience a wide variety of emotions. God has given guidelines to help us deal responsibly with feelings. Many people, however, simply reject certain feelings, such as anger, fear, grief, and sadness. Recovery from sexual abuse involves learning to recognize, experience, and share these feelings rather than rejecting them.

Anger

Many times sexual abuse victims will appear outwardly compliant and passive, but are inwardly filled with anger, hostility, and rage. The source of this seething anger might be the perpetrator of the abuse, the non-protecting parent, those in the school, church, or neighborhood who did not notice the abuse, or sometimes, those who created circumstances that "set up" the abuse. This intense anger is usually repressed and is often manifested by withdrawal, depression, or physical ailments.

It is important to define the difference between anger and bitterness and hate. Anger is a strong passion or emotion of displeasure. It is usually antagonistic, and is excited by a sense of injury or insult. Anger is a feeling of being out of control, vulnerable, and at risk of losing something very important. Usually one's self-identity is involved. Therefore, anger is often a "cover" for hurt, sadness, or fear. Anger is a powerful force. Locked inside, it can cause damage to self; out of control, anger can injure others emotionally, physically, or spiritually. However, anger can also be a positive force that provides motivation for change and healing.

Bitterness has different shades of meaning in the New Testament. It contains both the elements of "seized" and "pressed down."[1] When anger is suppressed, it is pushed down into one's "memory bank." This attempt to "fence in" the anger occurs because we think that by suppressing it, the anger will not cause hurt or loss of control. But when anger is repressed, we refuse even to accept the fact that we are angry; the emotion of anger is viewed as being "bad" or "wrong."[2]

Anger that is actively "seized" and "pressed down" causes bitterness. Lewis Smedes writes: "When you hate passively, you lose love's passion to bless. When you hate aggressively, you are driven by a passion . . . of hostility."[3] He goes on to describe how both forms of hate are malignancies that need healing, and that it is important to differentiate between anger and hate.

Expressing these feelings is necessary to facilitate healing. Scripture does not just teach us to stop being angry. It assumes, rather, that we will experience anger and urges us to learn how to express anger appropriately. Unless new patterns are learned, the pain of intense anger will often cause us to return to old patterns that remain from childhood: throwing things, withdrawing, yelling, transferring anger to others, blaming others, being hostile toward the body (over/under weight, over exercising, turning off sexually), being pessimistic, or rebellious, having judgmental attitudes, being sarcastic, or escaping to fantasy.[4] Often expressing feelings and confessing anger will disarm the feeling and its hold on the victim so that the abuse can be dealt with.

---

[1]James Strong, *Strong's Exhaustive Concordance of the Bible* (McLean, Va.: MacDonald Publishing Company), #58 in the Greek dictionary.
[2]Adapted from Anna Gates.
[3]Lewis B. Smedes, *Forgive and Forget: Healing the Hurts We Don't Deserve* (New York: Pocket Books, 1984), 39.
[4]Adapted from Anna Gates.

Many times Christians struggle with allowing people to express angry feelings, especially if that anger is directed toward God. In looking at Job's response to his devastating circumstances, Job 7:11 states: "Therefore I will not keep silent; I will speak out in the anguish of my spirit, I will complain in the bitterness of my soul." God did not shame or curse Job for expressing these feelings, but rather walked with Job through his trials. At the end of the chapter, God praised Job for being a servant who "spoke rightly" about God, He accepted Job's prayer, and He "blessed the latter part of Job's life more than the first."[5]

God's ideal guidelines for dealing with anger are found in Eph. 4:26–27: "Be angry but do not sin; do not let the sun go down on your anger, and give no opportunity to the devil" (RSV). Kenneth Wuest writes: "When guided by reason, anger is a right affection, so the Scripture permits it, and not only permits, but on fit occasion, demands it. . . . The words 'Be ye angry' are a present imperative in the Greek text, commanding a continuous action. This *orgē,* this abiding, settled attitude of righteous indignation against sin and sinful things, is commanded, together with the appropriate actions when conditions make them necessary."[6]

The sin of sexual abuse against a child is certainly cause for intense anger. Often the child is neither able nor allowed to express that anger, and as a result the sun "goes down" on this anger again and again. Thus, the Devil seizes the opportunity to convert righteous anger into hate, bitterness, depression, or psychosomatic illnesses in the victim.

Grief and Sadness

Grieving is a significant part of the recovery process for sexual abuse victims. Grieving is not only appropriate when a loved one dies, when we move away from intimate friends, or when we lose something very significant. Grief can also occur as the result of the fear of being separated from a significant other person. Grief can be a "gradual and painful process of with-

---

[5]Job 42:9–12.
[6]Kenneth S. Wuest, *Wuest's Word Studies in the Greek New Testament* (Grand Rapids: William B. Eerdmans Publishing Co., 1978), 113–114.

drawal of the emotional investment made in the lost person or thing."[7] Grief is the process of mourning *any* loss, such as the loss of expectations, the loss of dreams, or the loss of something we never had.

The losses that the abuse victim experiences are innumerable. A tremendous loss is experienced by victims who have lost their innocence, perhaps even being robbed of their childhood. When children are forced into adult roles to meet adult needs, they are deprived of normal childhood experiences like carefree play with friends or the freedom to develop healthy sexuality. Another loss that the victim must face is the loss of not having a protective or nurturing family or appropriate role models. When victims eventually realize how different things could have been, they come face to face with the realization that it really was as painful and deprived as they had inwardly felt. The loss of control over their own bodies and the invasion of the body without permission is cause for profound grief. Privacy, personal body space, personal boundaries—all are lost. The loss of value as a person cannot be measured, nor can we measure the loss of respect for self or the loss of trust of others. These major losses, and the myriad of others that each individual experiences, can culminate in the loss of personhood—the loss of self-identity and worth. This loss of personal identity can be a barrier to the realization of true identity because it makes it difficult to maintain a healthy view of God.

The victimized person will need to go through the grieving process for each perceived loss. Each must be "laid to rest," just as the death of a person must be mourned. The stages of grieving the death of a loved one are often reflected in the victim's grief over the sexual abuse. As Eccles. 3:1–4 emphasizes: "There is a time for everything, and a season for every activity under heaven: a time to be born and a time to die . . . a time to weep . . . a time to mourn. . . ."

Denial

Denial serves as a buffer or safety zone to shield a person from the reality of the pain of the abuse. "We need denial—but

---

[7]Stephen Grunlan and Daniel Lambrides, *Healing Relationships: A Christian's Manual of Lay Counseling* (Camp Hill, Pa.: Christian Publications, Inc., 1984), 105.

we must not linger in it," writes Joyce Landorf. "We must recognize it as one of God's unique tools and use it. . . .We do not need to feel guilty or judge our level of Christianity. . . . However, after . . . the initial danger has passed, we need not be dependent on it."[8] The tragedy of the situation for victims of abuse is that they have often, out of necessity for survival, been in denial for years.

Anger

Often a period of anger will follow when denial is broken down and the victim allows the reality of the abuse to come to the surface. Anger may be an expression of grief, and the expression of those feelings is crucial to the process.

Bargaining

In the intensity of the anger, the victim may desire to short-circuit the healing process, or desperately want the pain to be over, and may attempt some "bargaining" with God. Often the bargaining issue revolves around forgiveness: "God, I will forgive this person if you will take away my anger." Victims may state that they have forgiven the offender, but find no relief after doing so. Rather than realizing that the forgiveness process was prematurely short-circuited by a desire to avoid pain, the victim will beg, threaten, perform, or walk away from God for not keeping His end of the "bargain."

Depression

In his book *Healing Relationships,* Dan Lambrides states: "Reality has pushed through the defenses of denial, anger has depleted emotional resources, and bargaining has failed. At this point, depression sets in." A person may notice physical symptoms of depression, such as low energy level, changes in sleeping and eating habits, loss of sexual interest, or an unkempt physical appearance. Some psychological signs of this stage might include hopelessness, anxiety, loss of per-

---

[8]Ibid., 113.

spective, low self-esteem, emotional extremes in areas of dependency, feeling guilty, avoiding others or overreacting to situations or others.[9]

Acceptance: The Final Stage?

The process of grieving moves the individual through recognizing and acknowledging specific losses related to the sexual abuse. Grieving is facilitated by the expression of anger, grief, and sorrow, but acceptance does not end the pain of loss. Some degree of sadness will continue to remain because of the deep losses experienced by the victim. However, when one reaches the acceptance stage of the grieving process, his pain is no longer in control. The victim is able to let go of the "why" of the abuse, and will feel strong enough to move on in life. The church community needs to understand that grieving is not a one-time event, but a process that will continue as different issues, feelings, and memories surface.

Fear and Anxiety

The word *fear* comes from an Old English root word meaning peril. The feeling of being afraid or feeling that danger or evil is near can underlie many responses to being sexually abused. Often adult victims will be unable to give direct answers when asked about specific fears they may have. To understand the fears of the adult victim, one must look at the origination of these fears.

Fears originate during and after disclosure of the sexual abuse, and may continue for decades. Because the abuse may be physically painful, a child might not only fear the physical pain of the abuse but long-term physical consequences as well. Often the child has been threatened by the offender. Since most offenders are at least twice as big and much more emotionally powerful than the victim, the child has little reason to doubt that the offender can carry out any threats made.

Feeling powerless to stop the abuse and lacking control can trigger many fears—even the fear of death. When children

---

[9]Ibid., 121–142.

are forced or manipulated into sexual experiences, they do not have the inner strength to cope with the intense fears that accompany the abuse. When children experience the "damaged goods" fear, they feel that others can see that they are bad or ruined, and that no one else could ever love them.

"Everywhere I looked I was afraid" (Ps. 31:13, TLB)

Many fears are not experienced on a conscious level. Sometimes fears are expressed through nightmares or sleep disturbances. One woman had persistent terrifying nightmares of two geometric figures—a circle and a square. Later, in therapy, she was able to connect those nightmares with her sexual abuse experience. The circles and squares were patterns in the carpeting in her father's room. He had forced her face down on the floor, into the carpeting, each time he abused her. Her fears had been translated into the same recurrent nightmare for 35 years until she was released from those fears in therapy.

Fear is often manifested as anxiety, ranging from uneasy feelings or fears about what may happen to feelings of apprehension or dread. Anxiety can be experienced in many ways, three of which will be discussed below.

A Pattern of Panic

Panic anxiety is "free-floating" and not connected to any special circumstance or person. Victims who experience this type of anxiety are unable to say exactly what they fear, but they have a persistent sense of tension or dread. Such individuals are constantly "on edge" waiting for something dreadful to happen to them or to someone they care about. This kind of anxiety is distressing both for victims who have panic as a constant companion and for victims who experience panic descending on them "out of nowhere."

When anxiety is a constant companion, individuals will have trouble making decisions, have difficulty concentrating, and find it hard to follow through on commitments. Individuals often experience physical symptoms as well: muscle aches, headaches, nervous twitches, difficulties in breathing, racing heart rate, clammy hands, or insomnia.

When panic seems to descend "out of nowhere" in the form of a panic attack, victims experience an acute sense of impending doom and will actually fear that they are about to die, that they are going crazy or about to commit a terrible act. In addition to these physical symptoms mentioned above, the individual can experience dizziness, sweating, gasping for breath, shivering and a pounding heart. Because these panic attacks are unpredictable, individuals may not go out of their home, fearing another attack.

A Pattern of Phobias

Two factors define phobias. One defining factor is that the individual has an intense fear of a specific circumstance, person, place or thing. The actual feared object is usually not harmful, but carries some suggestion of danger—such as dogs, snakes, or heights. The feared object acts as a "trigger" of intense anxiety for the victim, and may even precipitate a panic attack. A second defining characteristic of a phobia is the behavior involved in avoiding the feared object. Many people will dislike the same objects that the phobic person dislikes, but the dysfunction is determined by the severity and degree of the reaction to the object. Individuals with phobias design their life around the avoidance of the feared object.

A Pattern of Obsession and Compulsion

Victims who struggle with thoughts or images that keep recurring in their minds, even though they may feel the thoughts are senseless or unpleasant, are said to be obsessive. Mild obsessions are experienced by everyone, such as a recurrent song or thought or feeling about something. Such obsessions pass. Of concern, however, is the involuntary dwelling on an unwelcome thought. One young mother, who had been a sexual abuse victim, had obsessive thoughts about sexually abusing her own child. Because these thoughts were extremely distressing to her, she sought help right away and was able to break the cycle of her obsessive thoughts.

A compulsion, on the other hand, is an action that the victimized person feels compelled to repeat over and over. The purpose of the repetition of the act is to relieve the anxiety felt by the victim. One sexually abused adolescent male responded to his anxiety by tapping his right foot three times, then his left foot three times. He did this each time he went out of his bedroom. While he viewed this ritual as "silly," he felt compelled to repeat it. Continuing the action relived his anxiety over what would happen to him if he didn't repeat it. A compulsion of excessive bathing or hand washing may develop in a person who feels "dirty" because of sexual abuse, or in the individual who feels "polluted" from having masturbated.

Christians usually have a great deal of shame about experiencing fears or anxieties. The Christian who has been a victim of sexual abuse will often feel like a "bad" Christian for even having fear. The church has traditionally applauded families whose children are well behaved and do all the right Christian behavior. These families, at the same time, may be very rigid, controlling, and perfectionistic in order to live up to the standards they believe are expected of them. This type of family system not only fosters anxiety-based problems, but may even create an environment for sexual abuse to occur.

Sharing Feelings

Because sharing feelings is a critical part of the healing process, sexual abuse victims will need a great deal of encouragement and support to begin to experience their feelings. A common fear of victims is that once they begin to uncover these intense emotions, they will lose control of themselves, "go off the deep end," or have a "nervous breakdown." Jan Frank, in *A Door of Hope,* suggests that while "going off the deep end" rarely happens, it is nevertheless important to have the expertise of a trained therapist when dealing with such deep emotions.[10] She recommends that victims obtain several counseling referrals from a reputable church or Christian agency. The victim needs to take the re-

---

[10]Jan Frank, *A Door of Hope* (San Bernardino, Calif.: Here's Life Publishers, 1987), 62.

sponsibility to question each referral over the phone to determine if that counselor is knowledgeable in the area of victimization. Jan Frank, herself an incest victim, cautions victims not to try to walk through their feelings alone. The therapeutic techniques that will be presented in the following material will best be implemented under the supervision and direction of a specially trained professional.

Tools to Facilitate Expression

Verbalizing

One of the primary goals of both individual and group counseling is to assist the victim to verbalize repressed or "stuffed" feelings. This often seems to be an insurmountable task to individuals who have denied feelings for many years. When verbalizing becomes difficult, many tools can be used to facilitate the expression of feelings. The method of expression is not important, but expressing the feelings is critical to the healing process.

Art Therapy

Different forms of art can be used to elicit verbal and non-verbal expressions of internalized areas of conflict. Using various art forms to facilitate sharing in a group setting can be a positive experience in relationship building between the individual, the group leader, and other group members. Sharing artistic creations facilitates support through positive feedback. The individual's artistic talent is not the source of enhancing self-esteem, but rather, self-esteem is bolstered by the fact that the individual is able to identify or uncover painful feelings, and able to express them to others. The actual drawing out of certain life experiences or scenes from the past can be a step in the maturation process needed to develop a healthy adult perspective.

A basic art tool might look like this:[11]

Individuals are given a box of crayons. Using different colors to represent different feelings, they indicate where feelings, such as anger, sadness, fear, or happiness, might be felt in the physical body. Sometimes individuals who report being unable to feel certain emotions—such as anger—will be able to discover that a tight jaw, clenched fist, or a knot in the stomach is actually a physical signal of anger. This may help the individual to more readily identify feelings that are often unexpressed.

Stick-figure drawings can be a powerful tool to help release feelings surrounding the abuse. The group members can be asked to draw out a painful scene from their life or from the actual abuse.

---

[11]Delores Selland, MA. (Artwork).

This drawing depicts a traumatic scene recalled by a 50-year-old woman. In this drawing, she is a 6-year-old child lying undressed on the couch. Her 19-year-old uncle is lying on top of her, abusing her, when her grandfather comes into the room. The grandfather sees her being abused, but does nothing, and walks nonchalantly out of the room.

Drawing this scene helped the woman uncover, and eventually release, the rage and betrayal toward both her uncle and her grandfather that had been deeply imbedded in her memory. The verbal expression of these powerful feelings is the catalyst that facilitated her healing process. Not only did she benefit from the expression of her feelings, but also from the validation of other group members who identified with her and supported how she was feeling. Other group members benefited by her sharing because it helped them get in touch with some of their own issues.

A variation of this technique is suggested in Frank's book. She suggests that it may be helpful for the victim to dig up old pictures and draw floor plans of the home in which the molestation occurred. Because some victims have multiple locations of molestation, or were abused by more than one offender, the counselor will need to be creative in helping the victim use this tool.

Word association is another artistic tool in which group members draw symbols that represent certain words, such as father, mother, home, family, sex, or love. One woman drew a circle in response to the word *mother*. To her, "mother" was a closed person who kept everyone out. This woman always felt excluded from mother's love and acceptance. A male victim drew a snow-capped mountain representing "father." He was able to express how this mountain was like his father—cold, distant and terrifying.

Writing poetry can help some individuals to express their feelings. The following poem from *Secret Shame: I Am a Victim of Incest* is an example of symbolism that clearly expresses the devastation of sexual abuse:

Watercolors

It was a watercolor painting—
bright yellow discovery

set jauntily beside sweet orange innocence.
With quiet strokes
came green familiarity
and a blue promise of love.
Then unexpectedly a streak
of black awareness—
    Innocence spoiled.
As red spilled across the paper—
passion on the edge
of purple fear.
Colors running together
until there was nothing left pure—
    not innocence
    not tenderness
    not even the joy of genuine passion.
Only a gray portrait
of the confusion and destruction
of a child become woman.[12]

Realistic or graphic prose can also be used to describe events. Graphic wording can provoke the reality of deeply intense rage and shame.

Inscription

Your words, jagged as broken glass, sharp as icicles,
Tore through the fine, white veil of my innocence
    —my childhood.
Your arms, your hands, plush, warmly stroking,
Hypnotic . . .
Have torn me limb from limb,
Razor-like, slashing beauty and virginity and
    femininity alike.
I am like an ugly circumcision
Done from pubis to lips.
A surreal Picasso nude—
chopped apart, re-formed in disarray.
I have been dipped in the sludge of
    your depravity,

---

[12]Martha Janssen, *Secret Shame: I Am a Victim of Incest* (Minneapolis: Augsburg Fortress Press, 1991). Reprinted by permission.

I am foul with your stench,
I carry a granite load—your guilt—
    upon my back.
Chained, it will not shake off.

—Elizabeth Moore McGonigle[13]

Family Sculpturing

Another form of expression is the use of family sculpturing. An individual "sculptor" selects other group members to represent those in his or her family. It is not essential that the chosen person look like the family member being represented. The chosen person represents, rather, the role played by that family member. Persons are arranged in position to one another for the purpose of depicting emotional closeness or distance; and roles, such as power, control, passivity, or helplessness. The "sculptor" then explains who is representing each family member and how those family members interact with one another and with the "sculptor." Often, individuals are unaware of perceptions of their family system until they participate in this exercise.

One 25-year-old woman, the "sculptor," placed one group member on a chair in the middle of the room, with another group member on her lap. Another person was positioned on a table, with her back to family members. A final person was directed to stand in the corner of the room and face the wall. The "sculptor" was overwhelmed to realize how isolated she was feeling from the rest of her family, as represented by the person in the far corner facing the wall. Her father was the most powerful person in the family, represented by the person standing "high up" on the table and was positioned with "his" back to the family, depicting his coldness and lack of involvement with the family. The unhealthy closeness of the mother and her younger daughter was shown by the fact the "mother" sitting in the chair had the adult "daughter" sitting on her lap. Feelings of intense rejection and a realization that she had never measured up to what she felt her mom wanted in a daughter were brought to the surface by this "sculpture." The usefulness of

---

[13]Used by permission of author.

this therapy tool can be maximized or intensified by having the "sculptor" role play and express feelings directly to each family member as if he or she were actually present.

Role Play

In another form of role play a person chooses a group member or the group leader to play the role of a person with whom they have unresolved feelings. One method involves the individual expressing his feelings directly to the person playing the role. The "role player" may or may not respond to the individual's feelings. Due to the fragility and vulnerability of most victim group members, this tool may be more appropriately used with the group facilitator playing the role.

Another effective variation uses an empty chair to represent the person with whom there are unresolved issues. This tool requires the victim to "pretend" that the "other" is present in the chair. It is particularly helpful in cases where the "other" person is deceased, unapproachable, or unavailable. Role play is a way for the victim to experience support, validation, and feedback following a powerful expression of emotions.

Written Expression

Writing can facilitate expression of feelings and can provide a vehicle for sharing them. Some individuals find it easier to write down their feelings than to verbalize them. Many people keep a daily journal that allows them to express feelings, document experiences, and evaluate progress.

Writing can be used for specific purposes in the healing process. Group members can be encouraged to write a letter to their offenders and others who were hurtful. Such letters need not be sent, but rather used as tools to help the victim express feelings. These letters are often brought to a group and read as part of the group process. An example of one such letter to an offender is given in Chapter 15: Step Seven, pp. 213–214.

Many have found it helpful to write a letter to themselves as children as if it were written by God. This often reveals their concept of where God was during their abuse. Individuals may write letters to God expressing their feelings.

Writing is also helpful when victims are encouraged to write a letter to their "inner child"—in other words, to the child they once were. (A structured example of this is found in Chapter 11, p. 154.) The victim will need to tell that "inner child" how he or she, as an adult, feels about that child. This tool often helps the individual by providing a vehicle for feeling the feelings repressed from childhood, standing back from the "child" and evaluating events with adult perspective, then reintegrating those childhood experiences into the whole person. One woman wrote:

Dear Neener, (my childhood nickname)

I know this letter is very late in time frame, but I also know that for your sake and mine I need to write it. There are so many things I want to say to you and that I want you to understand.

I guess I really want you to know that all the forms of abuse that happened to you were not your fault. You never asked to be hit, or screamed at, sworn at, cut down, or expected to be and do more than you were capable. Most of all I want you to know that it was not your fault that you were abused in sexual ways.

You were just a little girl. I know that it felt as if you were never a little girl. You always felt responsible for everyone. You wanted to protect your mom from your dad, and that was loving of you to want to do. But, Neener, you lost yourself. . . . All the blame that you got for the abuse and for all the times your dad left—it was not your fault. You could not have done anything more. It would not have helped if you were a better girl, and the sexual abuse still would have gone on even if you had physically fought harder. . . .

You were caught in a trap and there was no way out. You needed to keep all the secrets in order to survive and that was OK. You do not need to feel bad for that. You never could understand or figure out if it was OK to feel the way you did. You used to try to get your anger out on your dolls. You would talk, yell, and hit them just as mom and dad did to you.

You didn't understand what was going on with your body. All of the burning and discharges. You did not understand what they meant; all you thought was that you were bad and that somehow you were to blame. You were too scared to tell anyone because it was shameful. It's OK that you never told. At that point, you couldn't have emotionally handled it if everyone turned on you, just as you feared. And you always hoped and prayed that you would wake up the next morning and everything would be different. The sad truth and reality is that it never really got better.

I also want you to believe me when I tell you that it was in no way your fault that Jeff ran away. You felt responsible for him leaving because it was right after he raped you; but, Neener, it wasn't your fault. There was nothing you did to cause him to leave. It was his decision. You feel that if only you could have done something, then mom would have been happy, but that is not the truth.

Neener, you were very confused and you missed out on a lot. You lost your childhood, and you have a right to be angry and you need to grieve that loss so you can deal with the present and the future.

Please let yourself go and try to have less expectations of yourself. You do not need to put on all of your masks and act as if you have it all together when you really don't. Inside, you are emotionally just a frightened and hurt little girl. That little girl needs to be given permission to play, to cry, and to be angry. I want to give you that—something you never had. You can never have your innocence back, and that you can be angry at. But you have so much growing and learning to do. You need to start reaching out and asking for what you need. Start asking for help, hugs and support. You need to take risks and steps by letting everything out. You feel as if you are breaking, and it's scaring you, but it's OK.

You are just beginning to be really open and honest and look at all the traumatic secrets that you have held inside for so long. It is not easy but you can do it. Jesus is by your side.

I'm not trying to overwhelm you with things that you need to do, but I know that you need a direction and maybe this will help. Neener, one day you will be strong and healthy. Meanwhile, be patient with yourself; it will be a long process. You were abused for many years and you have a great deal of pain and anger to deal with. You need to believe in yourself and start to really love yourself. I know it is hard, but please remember that the abuse was not your fault. You were not and are not responsible. Take your time, please be patient, and remember you will get through this. Your past is only *a part* of you . . . it is *not all of you.*

Step Six: Accepting Responsibility

Step Six: I am accepting responsibility for my responses to being sexually abused.

Once a person has worked through the previous five steps, the group can assist in beginning to introduce elements of personal responsibility. This step is a very difficult but critical area to address, and for that reason it does not come early in the healing process. The cornerstone of the healing process is the recognition of the need for help from others and from God. Following that, the abuse victim will need to experience some measure of trust in the group leader and other group members. It is important that individuals feel that they are still loved and accepted even when others know the truth about them, and that they are not alone in their struggle. After some personal sharing by the victim individually and in the group process, it is appropriate to introduce personal responsibility.

At this point, the individual can begin to learn healthy ways to assume responsibility for his or her recovery.

Identifying Defense Mechanisms

People often attempt to cope with the residual problems of abuse by using defense mechanisms. Because of the intensely painful issues raised by sexual abuse, such self-protection is understandable. Drs. Lambrides and Grunlan point out that defense mechanisms often operate on a subconscious level[1]. These

---

[1]Stephen Grunlan & Dan Lambrides, *Healing Relationships: A Christian's Manual of Lay Counseling* (Camp Hill, Pa.: Christian Publications, Inc., 1984), 63–66.

defenses are a kind of self-deception and tend to deny or distort certain areas of reality.

Commonly observed defense mechanisms include:

1. *Rationalization*—victims convince themselves that the situation is not what it appears to be.

2. *Suppression*—victims cannot deal with the residual effects of the abuse, and so attempt to put it out of their minds.

3. *Repression*—victims block out painful events from their conscious memory.

4. *Denial*—victims refuse to acknowledge what has really happened.

5. *Displacement*—victims shift emotional reactions from one person to another.

6. *Reaction Formation*—victims replace an unacceptable feeling or motive with its acceptable, but often exaggerated, opposite.

7. *Projection*—victims project their thoughts and motives onto others.

While all people use defense mechanisms at one time or another, their excessive use can become unhealthy and dysfunctional. It is helpful to give abuse victims "permission" to respect their defense mechanisms as "survival skills" necessary for preservation earlier in their life. There comes a time, however, when individuals need to look at their defense mechanisms as present hindrances which inhibit taking responsibility to grow and experience the fullness that God would have for them.

Protective Shields That Block Recovery

Protective shields, or "survival skills," may have been taught to the victim by role-modeling. They may also have arisen out of the victim's creative attempts to survive. These skills, while providing protection when it was necessary, usually get in the way of the healing process. Part of taking responsibility for recovery involves the victim's willingness to identify and evaluate the use of defense mechanisms and protective "shields" and to make changes in areas that are necessary.

As part of the research for this book, 42 adult female victims of sexual abuse, participating in the BECOMERS program, completed a 40-question survey to reveal beliefs they held about themselves. The results of this survey will be integrated with the "shields" described below.

The Peacekeeper

Peace-at-any-price is a high cost to pay for the approval of others. This protection is used to shield the individual from risking disapproval. The victim who uses this shield as an adult is often praised, or at least approved of, for his or her willingness to "go along with" others. By constantly conforming to others' wishes and opinions, this individual actually becomes an anonymous person, lacking a personal identity. Of the 42 respondents in our study, 71% felt an acute need for others' approval to the point that they felt they could not be successful or happy without such approval. Beliefs that one must be loved by another person to be secure or happy (83%), or that to be criticized or to criticize is upsetting (71%), motivate many victims to use the shield of peacekeeping to protect themselves.

The Debater

An individual may attempt to prove his or her worth by creating "win-lose" competitions with others. This "shield" attempts to cover the shame issues of insecurity, lack of recognition, and sense of failure, and often succeeds in pushing others away. Because the individual has not learned to distinguish him or herself as a person of value, apart from achievement, being "right" yields a hollow victory and reinforces low self-image. Of the respondents in our study, 71% reported a need to excel in order to feel valuable.

A variation of this "shield" may show itself as intellectualizing. This "shield" is usually used to protect oneself from feeling or expressing true emotions out of a fear of being exposed as weak. Believing that one must not reveal or share feelings or weakness was reported by 38% of the respondents. Others can be kept at a distance by the use of intellectual conversation or apparent knowledge that "shields" the individual from an ability to experience close relationships.

The Dominator

The individual who uses this "shield" attempts to be in control by controlling him or herself as well as others. The dominating individual may display a desire to control other people's behavior, or even their thoughts and feelings. The highest statistic in the BECOMERS survey revealed that 85% of the respondents felt that they *should* be able to control their feelings. Many victims (69%) felt responsible to bring about changes whenever or wherever *they perceived* change was necessary. Individuals who use control or coercion with others usually feel that it is justifiable or reasonable in their circumstances.

A variation of the dominating "shield" is the egocentric "shield." In his book *Why Am I Afraid to Tell You Who I Am?* John Powell states: "It is almost a universal law that the extent of egocentrism in any person is proportionate to the amount of pain in him. . . . One cannot fashion himself to be the center of the universe and be content that others do not accept him as such."[2] Such individuals dominate others by constant reference to themselves in conversation.

The "Eternal" Victim

The individual who uses the "shield" of "eternal victim" has a twofold distortion of reality. This person does not have a true picture of him or herself, or a realistic view of others or others' motives. Because of this double distortion, such individuals have a difficult time trusting others, yet tend to blame others for their own unhappiness.

Victimized persons who are shielding themselves from personal responsibility in this way are usually aware of their inner hostile feelings but have developed delusions about the source of these feelings. These delusions, then, serve to create circumstances or imagined situations that affirm their inner feelings.

Maria struggled with victimizing herself through the use of a martyr-type behavior pattern. Her distorted perception of those who were trying to help her was demonstrated by her irrational responses when others confronted areas in her life

---

[2]John Powell, S. J., *Why Am I Afraid to Tell You Who I Am?* (25115 Stanford Ave., Valencia, Calif.: Tabor Publishers, 1969), 139–140. Used by permission.

needing work. When her therapist encouraged her to limit the number of counseling sessions per week to help Maria begin to break her dependency on the therapist, Maria jumped up from her chair, burst into tears, and accused her therapist of never caring for her and wanting to "dump" her.

Another characteristic that often coexists with this distortion is passive dependency. Some adult victims feel guilty for enjoying anything in life because they don't "deserve" it. Passivity is characterized by feelings of helplessness and being unable to control one's life. Of the victims surveyed, 45% responded that their moods were primarily created by factors that were largely beyond their control, such as the past, body chemistry, hormone cycles, biorhythms, chance, or fate. According to 52% of the respondents, their happiness was dependent on what happened *to* them, which again indicates their perception of powerlessness to change. This belief can lead to great difficulties with dependent relationships. Many times adult victims feel so unworthy of anything good that they may unknowingly choose abusive partners and passively allow themselves to remain in abusive situations.

The Fixer

The "shield" of the fixer covers inferiority, insecurity, and a lack of self-identity. This person derives self-worth from a need to be needed. He or she has a great deal of difficulty admitting a need for help, and in almost all relationships will view him or herself as the "fixer" and others as the "fixee." Such individuals most often attempt to "fix" others, rather than encouraging others to take personal responsibility for change. In addition, "fixers" usually assume responsibility for how others close to them feel and behave. The need to "fix" was reported by 50% of the BECOMERS respondents. Many victims use this "shield" to avoid dealing with their own issues or to avoid relating to others as equals.

Often, in Christian circles, people with needs are attracted to "fixers." "Fixers" are viewed as more spiritual because of their extensive "ministry" involvements, which in reality mask their own needs. An identifying feature of "fixers" is an assessment of their friends and primary relationships that reveal few, if any, healthy friendships. Wendy always seemed to find herself in the middle of other people's problems and crises. People seemed to look to her as a "savior" of the hurting and needy. The tragedy of this situation is that Wendy "medicated" her own needs by overresponsibility for the lives of others. Behind all the activity she remained a needy and unhealthy person.

The BECOMERS study revealed patterns of shame, inferiority, and perfectionism, all of which inhibit one from taking personal responsibility for change. Of those responding, 59% felt that rejection by someone close to them confirmed their defectiveness and they were therefore unlovable. Feeling like a failure, or inferior by comparison to others, affected 45% of the respondents, while 71% struggled with feeling "guilty," defined as having something wrong with them or being bad.

Clarifying Responsibility

Sexual abuse victims will need a great deal of encouragement to take risks, to give themselves permission to change, to experience failure, and yet try again. Some of the areas for which victims have chosen to take responsibility are:

- Responsibility for making healthy choices for self—changing abusive relationships;
- Responsibility to believe new "messages" about self to replace old messages—practicing positive self-talk;
- Responsibility to actively seek God for strength in the recovery process—appropriating Christ as source of identity to replace shame-identity;
- Responsibility to "let go" of blaming self for the abuse;
- Responsibility to work through conflict and not avoid it—attending individual and group therapy;
- Responsibility to be honest about feelings and "own" them, even though they may be painful;
- Responsibility to try new thinking and new behaviors, and to continue to keep trying;
- Responsibility to ask for forgiveness and/or make restitution for wrong choices in life that have hurt others;
- Responsibility to move toward more healthy relationships—for those who tend to be "fixers," letting go of controlling and over-responsibility; for those who tend to be

passive, assuming personal responsibility;
- Responsibility to forgive the offender (Forgiveness is discussed at length in Chapter 15: Step Seven.)

Resistance to Change: A Word to Leaders

A prerequisite for change is the individual's own need to identify areas needing change, and to take responsibility for personal growth, both in individual counseling and in group process. When individuals are encouraged or confronted about areas of personal growth, resistance is likely. One signal of resistance in a group setting is insincere agreement by the victim to the group leader's suggestion. Another signal is the presence of excessive emotion whenever a sensitive area is confronted. Victims may also try to engage a group leader in irrelevant arguments by trying to avoid painful subjects or following a suggestion with "yes, but . . ." A sullen, quiet response to the group leader's suggestion, direct antagonism, or a refusal to discuss the merit of the suggestion could signal active resistance.

Resistance is reasonable when the individual is open to considering what the group leader is saying, but genuinely cannot understand it. The solution to reasonable resistance is reasonable thinking. The trust in the relationship with the group leader is essential to this process.

Unreasonable resistance arises when the individual is unwilling to consider seriously or try biblical solutions offered by the group leader or counselor. Unreasonable resistance can never be overcome by rational persuasion. This kind of resistance is the primary source of power struggles in counseling. Leaders and group members can take the following steps to work through a time of resistance:[3]

1. *Identify resistance to assume responsibility.* For example, a leader might encourage a promiscuous group member to look at the choices she is making for which she needs to take responsibility. The leader might confront her by saying, "Maybe it's time for you to start saying no when your boyfriend wants sex. . . ." If she were to reject that idea, it would be necessary to identify her resistance: "You seem resistant to considering

---

[3]Material adapted from Anna Gates. Used by permission.

breaking off the sexual relationship you are having with your boyfriend. . . ." It is important to express genuine appreciation for how difficult it must be for the person to face the responsibility in this area. The leader might continue with, "It must be intensely fearful for you to consider this, especially if you think he will leave you. . . ."

2. *Help the individual reexamine her personal goals concerning areas she wants to change.* The leader might suggest, "Let's look at the goals you set up for yourself. You want to develop healthy boundaries, true intimacy with others and with God, and you want to recover from the shame of your past abuse. How does your choice to continue in a sexual relationship with your boyfriend move you toward or away from your personal goals?"

This process may take time, as the individual vacillates from wanting to make changes and the fear of those changes. The group members can be an invaluable support to one another by encouraging responsible changes. At times, a group member continues to make poor choices and is unwilling to change. If such resistance continues, however, a time may come when it may be necessary to terminate the group process. One might communicate acceptance of the individual as a person, while confronting the lack of responsible behavior in a statement such as, "I am committed to you as a person, and I care deeply for you. But I cannot enable you to continue in hurtful choices that are in conflict with your goals for yourself. Remember that you can return to the group process with a new agenda at any time."

3. *Encourage the individual to "move on," to let go of suppressed feelings, to begin the forgiveness process, to take responsibility for wrong choices or unhealthy relationships.* After the previous steps have built a foundation for trust and support, such encouragement can stimulate growth and change in the victim's life.

Many benefits can encourage individuals to take responsibility to share in the group process: bonding within the group, support and validation of one's feelings, affirmation of the individual as a person of worth, relief of some pain and shame, personal growth through risk-taking, gaining skills in listening to others, and honestly responding to those in pain. It is important for group members to realize that there are consequences for not sharing or for not taking responsibility for change. A decision not to share is a choice to not experience bonding with other group members. It can also be a choice to refuse group support, and to hold on to the pain in one's life. The safety provided by little or no risk-taking has the consequences of hindering personal growth or recovery.

Homework Questions

1. How do I define responsibility?
2. What things in my life do I feel are my responsibility?
3. Who is responsible for abusing me? What are they responsible for? Whom are they responsible to?
4. How much responsibility have I taken for causing the abuse?
5. Do I think I am more:
   a) over-responsible (take on what is someone's else's responsibility)?
   b) under-responsible (give up what is really my responsibility)?
   c) In what areas of my life do I see each of these responses?
6. Circle the following responses you have had to being sexually abused:
   Shame, fear, rage, anger, bitterness, self-hatred, distrustfulness of others, depression, manipulation of others, dishonesty, denial, chemical use, promiscuity, avoidance of men, bulimia/anorexia/overeating, suicidal thoughts/attempts, abusive to others. What other responses have you had?
7. Were some of these responses appropriate?
8. Do these responses continue to be appropriate in my life? Are there any that I would like to change?
9. Do I want to change any of these responses, or am I comfortable with them the way they are?
10. If I want to change any of my response(s), what would hinder me from taking responsibility for positive growth? What would help me take responsibility to make changes?
11. What is God's responsibility in my growth as a person?

Work project 2

(A note to group facilitators: Prior to completing this homework, the group members will need copies of the material presented in this chapter defining defense mechanisms and protective shields, pages 193–198.)

Work to be handed out to group members:

Part of the hardest "work" involved in the healing process is taking responsibility for things that can be changed and "letting go" of the things that cannot be changed. In order for us to take responsible care of ourselves, we need to identify defense mechanisms and protective "shields" that have previously been our survival skills but are now hindering recovery. Read the attached materials defining defense mechanisms and protective "shields." After reading the material, identify defenses and "shields" used in relating to others that you have learned from your experience of sexual abuse, from your family system, and from the way you feel about yourself.

1. Which defenses and/or "shields" do I find myself using?
2. What do these defenses and "shields" reveal about who I think I am?
3. How do these defenses and "shields" affect my relationships with others around me? How do they affect my relationship with God?
4. What is one step I could take to begin to take responsibility for change in this area?
5. What would hinder me from following through on the step I identified in #4?

For the last questions, consider this definition of victim/survivor:

A victim is one who was not in control and not responsible for what happened. A survivor has, by virtue of still being alive, survived, and, in continuing life, is now capable of having control and taking responsibility.

6. In my life right now, would I say that I think of myself as primarily a "victim" or a "survivor"?
7. What factors in my life reflect the answer that I gave to the above question?

◊ **15** ◊

Step Seven: Forgiving

Step Seven: I am willing to accept God's help in the decision
and the process of forgiving myself and those who have offended
me.

Forgiveness: A Crucial Step

Forgiveness is one of the most crucial, and often most mis-
understood, steps in the healing process. Within the Christian
community there is often a lack of understanding of the process
of forgiveness. This misunderstanding can result in offering
simplistic solutions to very difficult problems. Nothing about
forgiveness is simple! Even though theologically, forgiveness is
not a feeling, and does involve an act of the will, making the
choice to forgive and to say the words "I forgive you" can be
much more difficult than it appears.

Why Forgive?

Victimized persons need to understand that forgiveness is
only possible as God accomplishes it through them, rather than
thinking they have to do it themselves. The following poem by
Martha Janssen helps to express the feelings of a victim who is
struggling with the decision to forgive. She experiences feelings
of anguish over forgiving, which she likens to "jagged rocks."
These "rocks" may be hostility, rage, terror or fear. By expressing her feelings about being "rushed" into a forgiveness that
would not reflect a heart change enabled by God, she begins a
process of "knowledge and understanding" that leads her to
believe that one day she will not only desire, but actually be

able, to truly forgive. At that point she understands that God's command to forgive is not an impossibility for her.

Forgiveness

There are those who expect me to forgive
to let charitable kindness and reason
wash over me
    like a rushing stream
    over jagged rocks—
to forgive
now.

Seventy times seven—
the command may mean more
than first appears.
Not that one says "I forgive"
over and over and over,
nor that to will it
    makes it so,
but that one forgives
    as one loves—
gradually.
Forgiveness is a process
that begins with knowledge
    understanding
    believing in change.
I feel little charity now.
I can hope
    it may happen
    as I come to understand
    myself and you.

Seventy experiences and understandings
    times seven or seventy more.
I can believe I will forgive
    someday—then.[1]

In Matt. 18:21, Peter asks, "Lord, how many times shall I forgive my brother when he sins against me? Up to seven

---

[1]Martha Janssen, *Secret Shame: I Am a Victim of Incest* (Minneapolis: Augsburg Fortress, 1991). Reprinted by permission.

times?" The reply of Jesus gives insight to both the counselor and the victim who are addressing the issue of forgiveness. When Jesus tells Peter that he is not to forgive seven times, but rather seventy times seven, He was confronting Peter's superficial approach to forgiveness. Jesus is teaching Peter that forgiveness is not about "numbers" but a matter of the heart.[2]

People have many impressions of what "seventy times seven" means. Legalists might count the number of times they have said the words "I forgive you" and feel a self-righteous satisfaction at reaching the 490 mark. Perpetrators might use these verses to "preach" to the victims—after a quick "I'm sorry"—informing the victims that they are now responsible before God to forgive, thus leaving the victim revictimized by both the offense and the offender. Victims hear the words "forgive seventy times seven" and often weep, thinking that this means they are not to hold the perpetrator accountable, or that they should stay and continue to be victimized by an abusive relationship.

If we were to step back from these verses and view them objectively, however, one thing becomes clear. The question of forgiving "seventy times seven" makes such holiness beyond the reach of human ability. Peter's offer to forgive up to seven times is answered by Jesus' reply that it was not seven but 490 times that was required. In this way, Jesus was confronting Peter's self-righteousness based on his human ability to forgive seven times, and giving Peter a number so large that he would see his dependence on God for the ability to forgive from the heart.[3] This framework will help both counselor and victim as they look at God's command to forgive.

Moving Toward True Forgiveness

In teaching his congregation about "false" forgiveness, the senior pastor of a large evangelical church in Minneapolis shared the following insights. "False" forgiveness was defined as speaking the words "I forgive you" as words used to deny, minimize, or spiritualize the pain of abuse—a forgiveness void

---

[2]Pastor Dave Johnson, "Forgiving the Little Ones," based on Matt. 18:21–35, sermon tapes 83 and 84 (Minneapolis: Church of the Open Door, March 1989).
[3]Ibid.

of the release that restores broken relationships. "False" forgiveness often leaves victims feeling that they have not forgiven properly or that something is wrong with them or with God. Incompleted forgiveness also can be unsettling to victims when the hoped-for reconciliation does not occur. Pastor Dave Johnson illustrates three distinctions that contribute to both "false" and incompleted forgiveness.

Extended Forgiveness vs. Completed Forgiveness

Both the counselor and the victimized person need to understand the distinction between extended forgiveness and completed forgiveness. Completed forgiveness involves forgiveness from the heart of the victim, extended to the perpetrator, which is then received *with repentance* by the perpetrator for the fullness of the transaction that God intends forgiveness to accomplish. This does not always happen, however, and the victim will need to understand this transaction in order to understand what may happen if there is genuine forgiveness from the victim that does not meet with repentance from the heart of the perpetrator.

Jesus, from the cross, asked His Father to "forgive them, for they know not what they do." Jesus extended forgiveness to all, but that forgiveness was not received by all. The fullness of that forgiveness transaction did not occur in all to whom the forgiveness was extended. The thief on the cross responded to Jesus' extended forgiveness by receiving it with repentance, and the transaction was completed to its fullness.

When the victim extends that kind of forgiveness to the perpetrator, however, and it is not met with repentance and acknowledgement of the wound that was inflicted, forgiveness sometimes doesn't feel "full" or complete. While it is the desire of the Christian to want to extend forgiveness from the heart as Jesus did, it is also important to realize that, like Jesus, we may not enjoy the fullness of a restored relationship. We may experience pain such as Jesus felt as He looked out over Jerusalem and said, "O Jerusalem, Jerusalem . . . how often would I have gathered your children together as a hen gathers her brood under her wings, and you would not,"[4] and He wept and grieved

---

[4] Luke 13:34, RSV.

that He did not have a relationship with the ones He loved.

And then He released them . . . "Behold your house is forsaken. And I tell you, you will not see me until you say 'Blessed is He who comes in the name of the Lord.' "[5] That may be the end result of the victim's forgiveness of the perpetrator—it may be a "letting go" that falls short of restoration for which the victim no longer bears responsibility.

I'm Sorry vs. I'm Sorry

Many responses might meet the victim who is extending a heart of forgiveness toward a perpetrator. "I'm sorry" from the perpetrator can mean "I don't want to talk about this anymore," or "Drop it!" or "I don't want to look at your wound," or "I don't want to grieve over what I did." A victim who approaches a perpetrator may hear words like, "I'm sorry you feel that way," or "Well, I said I was sorry! What more do you want? You're the one that is supposed to forgive me, so do it!" or "Why are you bringing this up now?"

These indicators of lack of repentance often leave the victim feeling that the promised release and restoration of relationship did not occur, but not knowing why. The counselor needs to assist the victim in making the distinction between insincere "I'm sorrys" and godly sorrow coming from repentance that communicates messages such as, "I didn't know this had affected you so deeply," or "I am willing to hear your pain." The perpetrator who will listen without interrupting, defending or correcting the victim's feelings, will communicate a spirit of repentance; before a person can say he is sorry, he needs to know what he is sorry for. After having shared the wound, when repentance comes, when there is a groaning from the spirit that says "I am so sorry . . . ," there can flow the fullness of extended and completed forgiveness from the heart that restores and heals the relationship.

Intent vs. Impact

A third distinction that is needed by both counselor and sexual abuse victims is recognizing the difference between in-

---
[5]Luke 13:35, RSV.

tent and impact. Perpetrators may not have intended to inflict immeasurable damage on their victims, but in order for the fullness of forgiveness to heal the relationship, perpetrators must look at the impact of their actions. Victims must be able to express the full impact of what happened to them, from their perspective, in the process of forgiveness without being "shut down" by a perpetrator who says that he or she did not intend to do such damage. Again, as Jesus forgave from the cross those who knew not the impact of what they were doing, the victim forgives the fullness of the crime of which the perpetrator "knew not" the extent of the damage.[6]

Why Forgive a Perpetrator?

Why forgive? Particularly, why should someone who has been cruelly victimized forgive? It is understandable that sexual abuse victims find it extremely difficult even to consider forgiveness. Not forgiving may give the victim a feeling of being in "control" over the one who hurt them. It can be a way to try to "punish" the offender or to protect themselves from further injury.

At several stages in the process of recovery, however, victims may consider the possibility of forgiving their offender. For example, one unproductive reason to forgive in the early stages of recovery is to "get it over with" and to be done with the pain of the abuse. But forgiveness cannot be real or helpful if the pain has not been defined or discussed. Another example of inappropriate forgiveness is when forgiveness is used to "manipulate" God into making the pain go away. Demanding action from God—"I did my part, now you better come through for me"—sets up a victim for frustration and anger if the desired results do not follow. Another poor motive is to forgive in order to please someone else. It is counterproductive to personal growth to make outward confession with the mouth that is not the result of heart change.

Because God Says So . . .

Ultimately, the basic reason for forgiving one's offender is because God says to do so. However, it is important to present

---

6Johnson, "Forgiving the Little Ones," tapes 83 and 84.

a balanced view of Scripture when counseling abuse victims. Using the parable in Matt. 18:23–35, some counselors have drawn a parallel between the sexual abuse victim and the servant who was forgiven much who then refused to forgive a fellow servant. Ultimately, the king asks, "I forgave you all that tremendous debt, just because you asked me to—shouldn't you have mercy on others, just as I had mercy on you?"

Seeking the Balance . . .

In presenting a balanced view of Scripture, the victimized person needs to know what this "tremendous debt" was and who the king was who paid the debt that otherwise could not be paid. Isa. 53:4 states that Christ was that king—"acquainted with bitterest grief. . . . Yet it was our grief he bore, our sorrows that weighed him down. And we thought his troubles were a punishment from God for his own sins! But he was wounded and bruised for our sins. He was chastised that we might have peace; he was lashed—and we were healed!" "For God sent Christ Jesus to take the punishment for our sins and to end all God's anger against us. He used Christ's blood and our faith as the means of saving us from his wrath. In this way, he was being entirely fair . . ."[7]

This "tremendous debt"— this sin—does not refer in any way to the victim being involved in the abuse; it is the sinfulness we have each entered into spoken of in Rom. 3:23: "Yes, all have sinned; all fall short of God's glorious ideal; yet now God declares us 'not guilty' of offending him if we trust in Jesus Christ, who in his kindness freely takes away our sins" (TLB). Victims need to realize the "tremendous debt" they have been forgiven by Christ's substitutionary death on the cross. A penitent heart experiencing God's grace will be much more able to respond to the reality of choosing to extend that forgiveness to another, even to the perpetrator.

When counselors press the analogy further, comparing the victim with the king's servant who was forgiven much, but who would not forgive a fellow servant, i.e., the perpetrator, much damage can be done. It must be remembered that the unforgiv-

---

[7]Romans 3:25, TLB.

ing servant would not forgive his fellow servant a "small debt." Who of us could describe the violation of sexual abuse as a "small" debt? While the size of the debt is not the issue, it remains that the deeper the wound and the greater the pain, the more difficult and lengthy the process of forgiveness. Once again, it remains a matter of the heart.

Is Forgiveness "Fair"?

Another point of balance is to recognize that it will be difficult for the victim to see any "fairness" in needing to look at his own sin of unforgiveness because the sin of the abuse seems so much greater. At this point it will be of great benefit to the victim to be assured of the balance between the holy and just God who calls unforgiveness a sin and the merciful and grieving Father who says in Jer. 14:17, "Let my eyes overflow with tears night and day without ceasing; for my virgin daughter—my people—has suffered a grievous wound, a crushing blow."

We stand before God in total dependence on Him to resolve the paradox of His holiness and His mercy within the heart of the victimized person. The counselor needs to remember that he or she is responsible to present the truth and to model God's graciousness, while it is God's responsibility to convict the victim of the need to forgive and enable the victim to make that decision.

Making the Decision

A victimized person who has acknowledged the unforgiveness will then be faced with the decision to forgive. This decision, then, is a choice of the will, and is therefore not dependent on feelings. There is a fine line "between hypocrisy and following a scriptural prescription in the absence of emotion. It all has to do with motive."[8] Because God is concerned that the victim needs to "forgive your brother from your heart,"[9] the victim may need to ask God for a forgiving heart. Regarding such a request, Christ promises that He will be "close to all who call on him

---

[8]Jan Frank, *A Door of Hope* (San Bernardino, Calif.: Here's Life Publishers, 1987), 151.
[9]Matthew 18:35b, TLB.

sincerely. He fulfills the desires of those who reverence and trust him; he hears their cries for help and rescues them."[10] In this way, enabled by God's grace, victims can choose to forgive perpetrators in spite of a continuing struggle with feelings.

Processing the Decision

Feelings of anger and bitterness may return after forgiving the perpetrator but, while these feelings are entirely normal, such feelings do not invalidate the forgiveness the victim has extended to the perpetrator. When these feelings recur, the victim can share them with God and others with whom he or she feels confident and ask for help in once again validating and then "letting go" of these feelings. This process of emotional rest-recurrence-release may need to be repeated many times.

Liz was sexually abused by her grandfather from the ages of 2–14, and was verbally abused and neglected by her parents in a family system that was full of violence and anger. Liz had to ask God for a heart to forgive her many offenders, and now, after a process over three years, she writes:

> I've been able to forgive those who abused me. It was not a simple step of saying the words "I forgive you," but a process I worked through, first expressing my anger in the privacy of a counseling session toward those who had hurt me, and then realizing the abusers are victims as I once was. They are still suffering from their own lusts. They have offended not only me but also God. God has forgiven me, so I have forgiven them. . . . I still have scars. When they are touched, I hurt. But now I have tools to deal with the pain. Now I know God's love.[11]

Liz's story is an encouraging testimony of the power of God's Spirit to change a person's heart. But, Liz, like many abuse victims, did not begin the process of forgiveness with knowing God's love, but rather with a distorted view of God.

When Forgiveness Feels Impossible

Distorted images of God within the victim, often accompanied by anger at God, make it difficult for the victim to obey the

---

[10]Psalm 145:18–19, TLB.
[11]Jane McClain, "Overcoming the Trauma of Incest," *Virtue* (October 1988), 20.

scriptural directives just discussed. Early in recovery, most victims will see forgiveness as an impossible task. It is important to acknowledge the reality of this perception. Forgiveness does seem impossible. God has demonstrated for us, however, that forgiveness is more powerful than hate. Just as He cried from the cross, "Father, forgive them. . . ." so the victim cries out in forgiveness of the offender who "knows not" the impact of the abuse on the victim. In such identification with the victim, Christ demonstrates that forgiveness is more powerful than hate.

Results

In addition to obedience, there are several other practical reasons for encouraging victims of sexual abuse to struggle with forgiveness. One practical result of forgiveness is personal freedom. Not only was the abuse unfair, but it is equally unfair for the victim to remain in emotional bondage to the offender. Forgiveness can help break the bond of hate and bitterness between victim and offender. Once the abuse is shared and the feelings of devastation are identified, experienced, and expressed, it is counterproductive to continue to cultivate the initially appropriate anger. Anger that grows into harmful bitterness and unrelenting rage can destroy a person.

Because abuse distorts the use of power and control, another result of forgiveness is to regain the balance of power and control over one's own life. Forgiveness empowers the victim to experience not "a spirit of timidity, but a spirit of power, and love and self-control" (1 Tim. 1:7, RSV).

Forgiveness brings freedom—freedom from being controlled by the past abuse events, freedom from the emotional ties to the offender, freedom from the continual internal conflicts of bitterness and hate, freedom to become whole and enjoy the fullness of life. Maintaining these freedoms will be a struggle. The Galatians were instructed that it was "for freedom Christ has set us free." They were encouraged to "stand fast," and not "submit again to a yoke of slavery," which was, for them, living under the "law" rather than God's grace (Gal., Chapter 5). The "yoke of slavery" to abuse victims might include returning to an abusive relationship, trying to earn God's approval by religious performance, or shaming themselves if feelings of bitterness or hate recur. The abuse victim is to stand firm in newfound freedom.

The Process of Forgiveness

The following letter, shared by permission from its author, was written in the course of the BECOMERS group program by a woman who was both physically and sexually abused as a child. Her letter was used as an art therapy expression and was not sent to her father. Its purpose was to facilitate the initial step in the forgiveness process, and expresses with great intensity some of her personal pain.

Dad,

I want you to know that I've told. I've told the secret. Somewhere in the hazy part of my mind I remembered you telling me never to tell "or" . . . something horrible would happen—you'd kill me? I would die? "They" would take me away from you and mother, and then what would I do? Where would I live? These memories are hazy, but this I know without a doubt—you hurt me and you did it with malice and intention—it wasn't a mistake. "Hurt"—what a nondescriptive word to use for such influential circumstances. Tortured, ruined, tormented, destroyed, betrayed, hated—these words are better, but still not totally descriptive.

Maybe if I used words to describe how I came to feel about myself, about other people, about life, you would hear. But I know that is not possible—you hear nothing because you're deaf and see nothing because you're blind. I believe that is the way you want to be.

So you see, this letter isn't really for you—because you couldn't see the words or comprehend their meaning. It's for me—somehow forming these thoughts and saying these words makes me understand. And in understanding, I hope there is healing.

Hope. There is a word that is rarely in my thinking and talking. What you did to me left me without hope. Without hope there is nothing to strive for and nothing to live for. One who doesn't hope has no goals or dreams. He has no purpose. If someone has no purpose, there is no reason to exist. That is how I felt for as long as I can remember.

You never talked to me when you were "hurting" me, but your deeds screamed to me in unheard voices—unworthy, unwanted, guilty, garbage—I heard all these things and hundreds more. I've heard those words and voices as long as I can remember. They caused me untold misery and agony. The pain that I've existed with—not lived but merely existed—is so deep and black that it is indescribable.

You are guilty. Your actions and deeds have made my life agony. I've thought of destroying you, literally of killing you—but your pain would be gone and mine would continue. I've thought of publicly exposing you to all of the family, to all of your friends and business associates, but would that be enough? Somehow I don't think it would. I don't think there is anything I could do to you that could cause you the agony I've had. But believe this—if there was a way to get even, to repay, to revenge myself and be rid of you, I would do it.

I realize that your actions caused me to believe many lies. Those lies caused me to believe very destructive, hurtful things. These things I've believed have caused me to make many pitiful decisions in life. You not only affected me but you hurt my son by the things I came to believe.

But all is not lost for me because there is God. Somehow for some reason God has wanted me to live. He not only wants me to live but to live with peace and joy. How is this possible? It's possible because God loves and cares for me, and as much as I want to be healthy and whole—He wants it even more.

I believe God wants me to forgive. Why? You don't deserve it—God knows that. All the demons in hell know it. You don't even want it. So why would I forgive you?

For me! As I forgive you I let go of you—the sorrow, the rage, the memories, and gain peace—imperceptibly, minute bits at a time. I do not forgive because you deserve it, but because I deserve it and God asks it of me. I cannot live with my bitterness any longer, for it has nearly destroyed me.

I forgive you. I ask God to forgive you. I release you.

Beth

Beth's letter provides a guide to viewing the process of forgiving. It is obvious from Beth's letter that forgiveness is not the first issue that was addressed in her recovery process. Following two years of therapy, group discussion, and personal reading to acquire information about abuse, she has been able to lay the foundation for forgiving her offender.

Her first paragraph highlights the significance of revealing the "secret" of the abuse. As the letter continues, she is reexperiencing the memories of her childhood, once hazy but now clearly before her. The feelings are very deep and expressive of her torment, revealing her utter despair, agony, and hopelessness. She sees with harsh reality her own desire for vengeance.

She has also accomplished the difficult task of establishing that the offender is responsible for the abuse. With her words "You are guilty," she expresses her understanding of the part he played in damaging her life. She also demonstrates the confidence of knowing that she did not cause the abuse. This is an essential preliminary in the forgiveness process. Once she has assessed his responsibility, and emotionally "given" it to him, she is being freed to see areas of her personal responsibility to move toward forgiveness.

Forgiveness involves taking time to assess the fullness of the emotional damage, the false belief systems that have developed, the poor choices that have been made, and the anger and bitterness that remain. This assessment is almost always followed and accompanied by intense grieving over the many losses that have been experienced. (See also Chapter 13: Step Five, Grief and Sadness.)

Once a person has seen the need for forgiveness and identified all that needs to be forgiven, it is essential to know what true forgiveness is and is not.

In his book *Forgive and Forget: Healing the Hurts We Don't Deserve*, Lewis Smedes shares several insights into scriptural forgiveness. Often, victims are told by others that if they truly "forgive," then they will "forget" the abuse.[12] Smedes writes that individuals forget only what is too trivial or too traumatic to remember. Forgiving will enable the individual to experience healing of the lingering pain of the abuse, it will not result in forgetting that the abuse ever happened.[13]

---

[12]Jeremiah 31:34, KJV.
[13]Lewis B. Smedes, *Forgive and Forget: Healing the Hurts We Don't Deserve* (N.Y.: Pocket Books, 1984), 61.

In his article "The Possibility of a Healed Memory," Kevin Huggins writes:

> *Escape* from memories of the past was not scripturally advocated. Biblically, there was no warrant to believe that memory of its impact could be "healed" by forgetting or erasing the recollection of the event from one's mind. Paul's statement in Phil. 3:13, "Forgetting what lies behind, and straining toward what is ahead," is often misinterpreted. By "forgetting," Paul was not implying obliterating from the memory "what lies behind." In verses 4–8 of the same chapter, Paul clearly recalled some traumatic events from his own past (i.e., "persecuting the church"). It is clear "forgetting" these things for Paul amounted to a choice to reevaluate them (i.e., "But whatever was to my profit I now consider . . .") in such a way as to render them insignificant to obstruct movement toward his new goal of deepening his relationship with God. . . . Paul's own prescription for peace involved making one's anxieties and concerns known to God, rather than refusing to think about them at all (Phil. 4:6, 7).[14]

Neither does forgiving mean "excusing" the other person by being mushy and understanding. Smedes states that excusing is the opposite of forgiving. It takes only a little insight to excuse, but it takes grace from God to forgive. Before victims can forgive, they must stiffen their spine and hold the other person fully accountable. Precisely because there was no excuse for the abuse, the act of forgiveness requires a supernatural act.

Unhelpful Help

The process of forgiveness is sometimes short-circuited by well-meaning "helpers" who try to rush the victim. Sometimes this comes in the form of simple slogans as "You have to get on with things," "What's done is done" or "Let by-gones be by-gones." The process of forgiveness can also be short-circuited by quoting Bible verses ("All things work together for good"), by moralizing ("There's a lot to be learned from this") or preach-

---

[14]Kevin Huggins, "The Possibility of a Healed Memory," *Institute in Biblical Counseling Perspective*, vol. 1, no. 1 (A publication of the Institute in Biblical Counseling, Winona Lake, Ind., 1985), 77.

ing ("God means this for your good"). None of these shortcuts are helpful to victims because there are no shortcuts to forgiveness.

This urgency to forgive that is experienced by victims and their "helpers" is an attempt to smother the conflict. The pain of the abuse is difficult for both the victim and the "helper" to endure. Pushing a victim to forgive demonstrates a lack of understanding of the depth of the pain and the length of time needed for forgiveness.

Another unhelpful kind of assistance arises when victims are assured that instantaneous healing will occur if they "simply" forgive. If emotional damage remains, it can then be used as evidence that the individual did not "really" forgive the offender, or that the individual has an "unforgiving spirit." Ironically, this makes the abused individual responsible for any continued emotional distress. The victim is shamed and consequently re-victimized.

Jan Frank gives a vivid illustration of help that misses the mark in her book, *A Door of Hope*. Donna came to one of Jan's support groups and shared the following experience:

> I became depressed last week after a counseling session with my pastor. I'd finally gotten the courage to share with him all the events surrounding my background. I'd been molested from age 7 to age 15 by various men my mother brought home. I'd been raped repeatedly by my uncle and several cousins and eventually forced to have an abortion at age 15. I shared with my pastor how devastating these events had been on my marriage and about the depression that, at times, seemed insurmountable. When I told him about the anger I had toward my children and husband, the nightmares, and my inability to trust my husband, he stopped me short. He abruptly stated, "Donna, the problem is obvious. You have not forgiven those people who have in some way offended you. If you will right now forgive those people who in some way damaged you, you will be healed of all those symptoms you are describing." I wanted to forgive—in fact, I thought I had—but I was still experiencing those same difficulties. I went away in a state of defeat. I thought I was just not spiritual enough. I was destined to live my life in bondage.

As I went to work the following Monday I asked the Lord if He might show me something about forgiveness. Boy, was I surprised when He answered that very day! I'm a nurse and I work in the emergency room. A young man came in that day. He had just been run over by a truck and suffered a compound fracture of the leg. The bone was protruding, broken in several pieces. It took three doctors and two nurses four hours to get the man's bone set in a position to heal. The healing process would take anywhere from four months to a year. Even then, the young man might experience some difficulty in walking, and it could take several months more to obtain the full use of his injured leg. As I looked at this boy with his leg in a cast, I realized the Lord was using this to illustrate something profound to me. No one at any time approached the young man and said, "Son, I have good news for you. All you need to do is forgive the man who was driving the truck and you will be instantaneously healed." No one would be so foolish, and yet, how many of us approach emotional brokenness in that same simplistic manner?[15]

Sometimes abuse victims are told that if they truly have forgiven their offender, they should trust the offender once again and the relationship will be restored. This is neither true nor helpful. While the ideal situation might include reconciliation of the victim and the offender, several realistic factors must be taken into consideration. Because the return to a relationship is based entirely on trust, if trust has been violated, it can be rebuilt only over time, if at all. The victim of abuse must ask the question, "Can I genuinely trust that the offender will not abuse me again?"

Forgiving Ourselves

One of the most difficult areas of forgiveness involves forgiving self. While the abuse was hurtful to the victim, that abuse led to many poor choices that the victimized person made regarding self and others. Poor choices are often demonstrated in self-abuse or abuse of others, whether emotionally, physically or sexually abusing one's own children or spouse, or abusing

---

[15]Frank, *A Door of Hope*, 133.

self with chemicals, sex, food, workaholism, or perfectionism. The scars of these past sins must not be allowed to haunt the victimized individual in the present and in the future.

Forgiving ourselves means being honest about our own humanness, and realizing that our choices were influenced by sins committed against us. While this is not intended to minimize or "justify" hurting ourselves or others, forgiving self requires courage, compassion and the ability to see ourselves the way God sees us. Victimized persons must forgive themselves for repeating their victimization, or for not knowing how to protect their own children. They may have to forgive their bodies for responding physiologically to the abuse, or for "betraying" them. Forgiveness should be sought for specific actions and for one action at a time. We do not ask God to forgive us for being cruel, hateful, or stupid, but rather for actions of cruelty, hatefulness, or wrong choices. This distinction differentiates between true guilt, which is about behavior, and shame, or false guilt, that attacks one's identity and value as a person. Smedes writes that if you should dare to forgive yourself, it would be a signal to the world that God's love is a power within you.[16] Forgiving yourself will help to energize personal healing and help focus on further growth.

Forgiving God

Many people struggle intensely with bitterness and anger toward God because He is blamed for allowing the abuse. As Elizabeth prayed in Chapter 4, many child victims begged God repeatedly to stop the abuse but the abuse continued. This pain can increase through the years and often culminates in rage toward God. This inner conflict creates a dichotomy within the Christian who feels he "should" love God, but feels he cannot. Often, individuals will repress their true feelings toward God. Overtly hating God can take the form of flagrant violations of His moral laws and outright defiance of scriptural truth. Sometimes these feelings are expressed indirectly to God by hating His gifts, His world, or self.

Smedes illustrates a passive hatred toward God with such

---

[16]Smedes, *Forgive and Forget*, 105.

signals as resenting good things happening to friends, stifling every happy impulse, or shutting our eyes to every reason we have for being glad to be alive. Often Christians behave like Jeremiah, who, when he felt really let down by God, turned his hatred on himself. Hating God's most precious gift of life can be a believer's way of hating God.

To help relieve abuse victims of hidden rage against God, the counselor can assist them to identify disappointment or feelings of being unfairly hurt by giving permission to express those feelings to the counselor, to others in their group, and directly to God in prayer. Philip Yancey addresses this issue in his book, *Disappointment With God*: "Knowledge is passive, intellectual; suffering is active, personal. No intellectual answer will solve suffering. Perhaps this is why God sent His own Son as one response to human pain, to experience it and absorb it into himself. The Incarnation did not 'solve' human suffering, but at least it was an active and personal response."[17] Dr. Paul Brand, responding to the question, "Where is God when it hurts?" replies, "He is in you, the one hurting, not in it, the thing that hurts."[18] "Would it be too much " writes Yancey, "to say that, because of Jesus, God understands our feelings of disappointment with Him? How else can we interpret Jesus' tears, or His cries from the cross . . . that dreadful cry, 'My God, my God, why have you forsaken Me?' "[19]

Within helpful and supportive relationships, the individual may discover rage or even hatred toward God that has remained hidden for years. Because this is a critical time in the victim's spiritual recovery, these feelings should not be stifled by the counselor, the group leader, or group members who might be trying to "defend" God and "fix" the relationship. Forgiveness—even "forgiving" God!—begins with the expression of intense emotions. The fullness of the forgiveness process—identifying and expressing feelings about the abuse, looking at the command to forgive, seeing the need to forgive, making the decision to forgive, and experiencing progressive changes in feelings—will be completed in time. One member of BECOMERS,

---

[17]Philip Yancey, *Disappointment With God: Three Questions No One Asks Aloud* (Grand Rapids: Zondervan Books, 1988), 192.
[18]Ibid., 183.
[19]Ibid., 128.

a daughter of missionary parents, and abused by an elder in the church, was inwardly struggling with hate toward God. She wrote in response to a homework assignment:

> Thank you so much for this group. It is so freeing to have a place where people accept me, and I can say all these feelings out loud, and no one is going to condemn me, or better yet, no one is going to throw verses at me or try to argue with me. Thank you for saying it's OK to be where I am—that makes me want to change more than anything.

Homework Questions

1. What does the word "forgiveness" mean to me?
2. What part do I feel that forgiveness plays in my healing process?
3. Who has ever hurt or offended me, treated me unjustly or violated my rights? How do I feel toward them?
4. What do I do with those feelings?
5. How do I feel about forgiving those who have offended, abused, or rejected me?
6. List some of the basic needs of children. Which of those needs were not met for me in my childhood?
7. Who was responsible for meeting those needs, but did not?
8. How do I feel toward those persons?
9. Could I consider forgiving those persons?
10. What have I been taught about forgiving those who have offended me?
11. Have I tried doing what was taught? Did it work?
12. How do I feel about the statement "forgive and forget"?

Forgiving self

13. What actions of mine have been hurtful to others?
14. What other choices have I made that necessitate my taking responsibility to ask forgiveness?
15. In what areas am I unable to forgive myself? What is it about these areas that make them difficult for me to accept God's forgiveness?

Body image

With a focus on forgiveness, work through the following questions as they relate to body image.

16. What parts of my body do I have trouble accepting?
17. Who were the people in my life who "put down," shamed, or caused harm to certain parts of my body? How did they do this?
18. Am I experiencing anger, fear, sadness, disgust or other feelings toward certain parts of my body?
19. If I were to talk to those parts of my body, what would I say to them? What would those body parts answer back to me?
20. How do I think God feels about those parts of my body?
21. What would enable me to forgive those parts of my body that have caused me shame or pain?
22. What would enable me to forgive the people who shamed or hurt my body?

Forgiving God

23. Write about feelings toward God.
24. What are issues in my Christian walk that cause me concern which might be related to feelings about God?
25. Write a letter to God expressing current adult feelings about Him.
26. Write a letter to God expressing past childhood feelings about Him.
27. What would God write back to me?
28. What seems to get in the way of my "forgiving" God?
29. What might help enable me to "forgive" God?

◊ **16** ◊

Step Eight: Maturing in Relationship With God and Others

Step Eight: I have determined to mature in my relationship to God, and those around me.

Maturing in Relationship With God

To mature in a relationship with God means, in part, to see Him as He really is. It also means to experience and gradually replace distorted images of God with the truth about who He is. Maturity, then, is the process of walking with God in one's daily life based on that reality.

This step is usually one of the final steps in the recovery process. To experience mature and healthy relationships on a horizontal level with others requires a foundational vertical relationship with God. In 1 John 3:1–2 we have a picture of a mature relationship with God, showing first, God's view of us, and then, our view of ourselves in Him.

The book of First John is attributed to the Apostle John who personally walked with Jesus and experienced being one "whom Jesus loved."[1] The tone of John's letter implies that he is an old man, mature and secure in his faith. He writes to unidentified readers, a general letter to Christians at large.

Consider the incredible love that the Father has shown us in allowing us to be called "children of God"—and that is not just what we are called, but what we are. Our heredity on the godward side is no mere figure of speech—which explains why the world will no more recognize us than it

---

[1]John 13:23, RSV.

223

recognized Christ. Oh, dear children of mine (forgive the affection of an old man), have you realized it?

Here and now we are God's children. We don't know what we shall become in the future. We only know that, if reality were to break through, we should reflect His likeness, for we should see Him as He really is. (1 John 3: 1–2, Phillips)

Abused persons who have seen God only as a harsh punitive father-figure standing eagerly waiting to "judge" them need to focus on scriptures that emphasize God's love, mercy, compassion and grace. This will enable them to get a more balanced picture of God and greatly assist their relationship with Him. Dr. David Seamands writes in *Healing of Memories* that many emotionally damaged people find themselves "consistently selecting Bible passages which emphasize wrath, punishment, and the unpardonable sin. Unless Christian workers truly understand the dynamics of this, they will not be able to help these damaged persons. They will actually harm them, overloading more oughts and guilts upon them by giving them the spiritual disciplines of Bible reading and prayer."[2]

The following illustration, adapted from the teachings of Dr. Seamands, illustrates this concept. As Dr. Seamands explains, it is extremely important to understand the connection between what one *hears* about God and what one actually *feels* about God. As God's truth is "funneled" into the cognitive intellect, we often expect the mere transmission of that truth to directly penetrate the heart and produce needed changes in a person's life. The person with a shame filter, however, will not experience the truth about who God is. As illustrated, because a relationship with God has been distorted by unhealthy interpersonal relationships, usually in childhood or adolescence, one's relationship with God "funnels" through a "shame filter" and is distorted.

The distorted truth about God first comes in through the outside, but is then transmitted from within. Such distortion becomes a pattern of life. "We could liken their condition to a kind of spiritual paranoia," states Dr. Seamands. "Paranoid per-

---

[2]David A. Seamands, *Healing of Memories* (Wheaton, Ill.: Victor Books, 1985), 103.

Receiving God's Truth

God's Truth

Shame Filter

What we expect
to happen . . .

God's truth
produces fruit

What happens . . .

Damaged reception of
truth due to the
shame from unhealthy
interpersonal relationships.

sons can take the most loving, affirming statements and twist
them into insults, rejections, and even threats."[3] The good news
becomes the bad news—the loving, caring God of Scripture be-

[3]Ibid., 103.

comes, at best, indifferent, and at worst, hateful.

Dr. Seamands writes that in spite of our "most rigorous Christian disciplines," we will "never find lasting 'righteousness, peace, and joy in the Holy Spirit' (Rom. 14:17) until we find a Christlike God, the kind of God, who, like Jesus, tells us He no longer considers us 'slaves' but 'friends' (John 15:15)."[4]

BECOMERS group members are encouraged to do creative Scripture homework in which they take a passage of scripture and personalize it, describing God's reality to them. This is a valuable tool in helping individuals replace distorted images of God with His truth, as demonstrated in this example of creatively personalizing 1 Cor.13:4–8:

Because God Loves Me

Because God loves me, He is slow to lose patience with me.

Because God loves me, He takes the circumstances of my life and uses them in a constructive way for my growth.

Because God loves me, He does not treat me as an object to be possessed and manipulated.

Because God loves me, He has no need to impress me with how great and powerful He is because *He is God*, nor does He belittle me as His child in order to show me how important He is.

Because God loves me, He is for me. He wants to see me mature and develop in His love.

Because God loves me, He does not send down His wrath on every little mistake I make, of which there are many.

Because God loves me, He is deeply grieved when I do not walk in the ways that please Him because He sees this as evidence that I don't trust Him and love Him as I should.

Because God loves me, He rejoices when I experience His power and strength and stand up under the pressures of life for His name's sake.

Because God loves me, He keeps on trusting me when at times I don't trust myself.

---

[4]Ibid., 104.

Because God loves me, He never says there is no hope for me; rather, He patiently works with me, loves me and disciplines me in such a way that it is hard for me to understand the depth of His concern for me.

Because God loves me, He never forsakes me even though many of my friends might.

Because God loves me, He stands with me when I have reached the rock bottom of despair, when I see the real me and compare that with His righteousness, holiness, beauty, and love. It is at a moment like this that I can really believe that God loves me.

Yes, the greatest of all gifts is God's perfect love.[5]

Maturing in Relationship With Others

Mature relationships depend on the foundation of a Christ-based identity and a personal realization and appreciation for one's uniqueness and specialness as an individual. Often, abused individuals have learned to derive their identity from others and have not experienced relationships with a potential for personal growth and maturity. Healthy relationships are not blocked by dependencies on others, by passivity, or by aggression. Rather, healthy mature relationships are based on the ability to be assertive, that is, to be both respectful and honest with self and others. (See Chapter 12 on issues of identity, and dependency issues in Chapter 6, pp. 81–82.)

Passivity

When victims adopt a passive role in relationships, they actually violate their own value by failing to express honest feelings, thoughts, and beliefs. This consequently permits others to violate them. Passivity is also demonstrated by expressing thoughts and feelings in such an apologetic or self-effacing manner that others can easily disregard them. The "messages" communicated by passivity in relationships are often messages like: "I don't count; you can take advantage of me," or "My feelings

---

[5]Pastor Dick Dickinson, Inner Community Counseling Center, Long Beach, Calif.

don't matter; only yours do," or "I'm nothing; you are superior."

Many passive relationships are unhealthy because the individuals involved want to be "nice." The following excerpt from *Creative Aggression* explains:

> "Nice" behavior eventually has a "price" for both the "nice" guy and the person or persons involved with him. It is alienating, indirectly hostile, and self-destructive because:
>
> 1. The "nice" guy tends to create an atmosphere that causes others to avoid giving him honest, genuine feedback. This blocks his emotional growth.
>
> 2. "Nice" behavior will ultimately be distrusted by others. That is, it generates a sense of uncertainty and lack of safety in others, who can never be sure if they will be supported by the "nice" guy in a crisis situation that requires an aggressive confrontation with others.
>
> 3. "Nice" guys stifle the growth of others. They avoid giving others genuine feedback, and they deprive others of a real person to assert against. This tends to force others in the relationship to turn their aggression against themselves. It also tends to generate guilt and supress feelings in others who are intimately involved and dependent on him.
>
> 4. Because of his chronic "niceness," others can never be certain if the relationship with a "nice" guy could endure a conflict or sustain an angry confrontation if it occurred spontaneously. This places great limits on the potential extent of intimacy in the relationship by putting others constantly on their guard.
>
> 5. "Nice" behavior is not reliable. Periodically, the "nice" person explodes in unexpected rage, making those involved with him shocked and unprepared to cope with it.
>
> 6. The "nice" guy, by holding his aggression in, may pay a physiological price in the form of psychosomatic problems and alienation.
>
> 7. "Nice" behavior is emotionally unreal. It puts severe limitations on all relationships, and the ultimate victim is the "nice" person himself.[6]

---

[6]George Back and Herb Goldberg, *Creative Aggression*.

Aggression

The use of aggression in relationships violates the rights of others and has domination as its goal. Aggression in relationship implies that someone will win and the other person will lose. The person who loses is humiliated, degraded, belittled, or overpowered in an aggressive relationship. The loser then becomes less able to express his feelings or his needs. Those who behave aggressively in relationships are usually dishonest about their own inner feelings and attempt to reduce their own anxiety by blaming others. Aggressive relationships communicate such messages as "This is what I think —you're stupid for believing differently," or "This is what I want   what you want isn't important," or "This is what I feel, and your feelings don't count."

Passive Aggression

When individuals express indirectly their hostility to others, they are being both passive and aggressive in their relationships. For example, negativism, disinterest, procrastination, or sullenness can be passive attempts to cover aggressive feelings. Passive aggressiveness is dishonest in that trickery, seduction, or manipulation is used. The other person is unaware of the anger or "getting even" intent because the passive aggressive relationship is so indirect.

Assertiveness

Mature relationships can grow and be nurtured through assertiveness. The two components of assertiveness are honesty and respect. Assertiveness involves standing up for one's thoughts, feelings and beliefs in a direct, honest, and appropriate way that does not violate another person's rights or show disrespect.

Learning relationship skills can be a difficult, trial-and-error learning process for those victimized by sexual abuse. Individuals are often passive in some relationships and aggressive or passive aggressive in others. Many victims do not have a no in their vocabulary, because no never meant no when they said it, or because their no was overruled. Marge had been sexually abused by her grandfather as a child. As an adult, difficulties arose in her marriage, her husband left her, and she remained separated from him for five years without finalizing a divorce.

Marge's husband made a practice of coming to "visit" her about every six months. He would call one of Marge's friends and tell her to inform Marge that he was coming. Marge would dutifully leave the door open at the appointed time. He would return to the house, verbally and physically abuse her, sexually use her, and then leave, only to return again in a few months to repeat the cycle.

Marge had adopted a passive role in this abusive relationship, and was honestly unaware that she could say no to such demeaning and hurtful actions. It took many months of counseling and BECOMERS group sessions to strengthen her to the point where she valued herself enough to not allow him to misuse her so disrespectfully and to say no.

Assertiveness is also a difficult skill to learn for those who use aggression in relationships. Maturing in relationships involves taking responsibility for the inappropriate use of power in attempting to control others. (See also "Abuse of Power," Chapter 6, pp. 69–71.) Sam had been severely abused by several significant male father-figures during his childhood. He had "learned" that to show any emotions was weakness, and that to be truly masculine he had to be macho, physically aggressive, and always "win" in any relationship. In group sessions, Sam found it almost impossible to relate to the other men who were sharing feelings of hurt or fear. He even threatened some of the men with physical violence if they showed signs of emotion.

A group exercise helpful in learning assertiveness skills involves two persons in a role play. This can be conducted with a large group of individuals. The group members are broken down into pairs. One of them attempts to "sell" a product to his partner. The partner's task is to refuse to buy the product by calmly, yet persistently, refusing without becoming argumentative or angry. This might involve repeating "No, thank you. I'm not interested." When asked again, the buyer simply repeats in a calm manner, "No, thank you. I'm not interested." After several minutes, the roles are reversed, so that individuals are both buyer and seller.

This rather arbitrary exercise may seem awkward and stilted

at first, but practice of this principle as a communication skill will allow individuals to feel comfortable in ignoring manipulative, verbal exchanges and irrelevant logic while maintaining their original point. Once group members have learned the skill and have gained confidence in using it, they can then begin to apply it in real-life situations.

Another assertiveness exercise, again using pairs of individuals, is a role play involving another response skill. In this exercise, the "seller" tries to manipulate the "buyer" with negative criticism. The buyer, instead of simply repeating the same answer over and over, this time acknowledges that, even though there may be some truth to what the seller is saying, his decision is, nevertheless, no. For example, the buyer says calmly, "Yes, I do believe the product is worth the price. However, I am not interested." When the seller persists, the buyer might respond, "It is probably true that my children could benefit from your product, but I am not interested." After practice in a simulated situation and learning to feel relaxed using this skill, group members become more comfortable in receiving criticism without feeling defensive or pressured to give in. Members demonstrate personal integrity and honesty by not doing something they do not want to do. They demonstrate respect for themselves and others as equals by not allowing the other to be in control of their personal decisions. This skill is invaluable to sexual abuse victims in maintaining a sense of balance and control in everyday situations.

Personal Boundaries

Individuals who have experienced sexual abuse have had their personal boundaries violated. Even as adults, they are often unaware of appropriate personal boundaries. One such boundary is in the area of saying no to physical expressions of affection they do not desire. While touch can be very affirming and supportive, the abuse victim needs to learn to say yes or no to physical touch, such as a hug, based on self-worth rather than on the request or need of the other person. There are extremes in boundary issues, such as those who touch, hug, or kiss others without regard to their boundaries, or those who allow others to touch, hug, or kiss them when they don't want to. Another extreme in personal boundaries is the fear of any touch or closeness.

The role of personal boundaries is to assist individuals in recognizing where they are passive in letting others cross their personal space, where they are aggressive in violating another's space, or where they are isolating themselves by refusing even nurturing contact from trustworthy others. (See also "Social Isolation," Chapter 6, pp. 75–76, and "Blurred Boundaries, pp. 79–81.

Homework Questions

1. What is the difference between assertiveness and aggressiveness?
2. What does passive aggressive mean?
3. What are some of the reasons that make people hesitant to share their thoughts, beliefs, or feelings in their relationships with others? What are my reasons?
4. In which of my relationships do I take . . .
   a. a passive role;
   b. an aggressive role;
   c. a passive aggressive role.
5. I am involved in many different relationships—spouse, friend, co-worker, parent, child, boss/employee, group member. In which of these relationships do I feel most comfortable to . . .
   a. ask for assistance;
   b. refuse a request;
   c. express my feelings about something important to me.
   In which of these relationships do I feel least comfortable to . . .
   a. ask for assistance;
   b. refuse a request;
   c. express my feelings about something important to me.

An assertiveness inventory is provided at the end of this section to help in evaluating an individual's level of assertiveness.

Boundary issues

6. Recently, my personal boundaries were violated by . . .
   I felt . . .

I did . . .

Next time, I could . . .

7. Recently, I violated the personal boundaries of . . .

I was unaware of . . .

I felt . . .

He/she felt . . .

Next time, I could . . .

Relationships

8. What is my current relationship with God like? Is there anything I would like to change?

9. What are my current significant relationships like?

10. How have I matured in these relationships so far in my healing process?

11. Am I involved in any unhealthy relationships? What could I change?

Assertiveness Inventory[7]

The following questions will be helpful in assessing your assertiveness. This tool is not designed to be "scored," but rather to help indicate areas of difficulty in maintaining assertive behavior. Be honest in your responses. All you have to do is draw a circle around the number that describes you best. For some questions the assertive end of the scale is at 0, for others at 4. Key: 0 means "no" or "never"; 1 means "somewhat" or "sometimes"; 2 means "average"; 3 means "usually" or "a good deal"; and 4 means "practically always" or "entirely."

1. When a person is highly unfair, do you call   0 1 2 3 4
   it to his attention?

2. Do you find it difficult to make decisions?   0 1 2 3 4

3. Are you openly critical of others' ideas,   0 1 2 3 4
   opinions, behavior?

4. Do you speak out in protest when someone   0 1 2 3 4
   takes your place in line?

5. Do you often avoid people or situations for   0 1 2 3 4
   fear of embarassment?

---

[7]Assertiveness Inventory, Dr. Paul Mauger.

6. Do you usually have confidence in your own judgment?   0 1 2 3 4

7. Do you insist that your spouse or roommate take on a fair share of household chores?   0 1 2 3 4

8. Are you prone to "fly off the handle"?   0 1 2 3 4

9. When a salesman makes an effort, do you find it hard to say "No" even though the merchandise is not really what you want?   0 1 2 3 4

10. When a latecomer is waited on before you are, do you call attention to the situation?   0 1 2 3 4

11. Are you reluctant to speak up in a discussion or debate?   0 1 2 3 4

12. If a person has borrowed money (or a book, garment, something of value) and is overdue in returning it, do you mention it?   0 1 2 3 4

13. Do you continue to pursue an argument after the other person has had enough?   0 1 2 3 4

14. Do you generally express what you feel?   0 1 2 3 4

15. Are you disturbed if someone watches you at work?   0 1 2 3 4

16. If someone keeps kicking or bumping your chair in a movie or a lecture, do you ask the person to stop?   0 1 2 3 4

17. Do you find it difficult to keep eye contact when talking to another person?   0 1 2 3 4

18. In a good restaurant, when your meal is improperly prepared or served, do you ask the waiter/waitress to correct the situation?   0 1 2 3 4

19. When you discover merchandise is faulty, do you return it for an adjustment?   0 1 2 3 4

20. Do you show your anger by name-calling or obscenities?   0 1 2 3 4

21. Do you try to be a wallflower or a piece of the furniture in social situations?   0 1 2 3 4

22. Do you insist that your landlord (mechanic, repairman, etc.) make repairs, adjustments or replacements which are his responsibility?   0 1 2 3 4

23. Do you often step in and make decisions for others?   0 1 2 3 4

24. Are you able openly to express love and affection? 0 1 2 3 4

25. Are you able to ask your friends for small favors or help? 0 1 2 3 4

26. Do you think you always have the right answer? 0 1 2 3 4

27. When you differ with a person you respect, are you able to speak up for your own viewpoint? 0 1 2 3 4

28. Are you able to refuse unreasonable requests made by friends? 0 1 2 3 4

29. Do you have difficulty complimenting or praising others? 0 1 2 3 4

30. If you are disturbed by someone smoking near you, can you say so? 0 1 2 3 4

31. Do you shout or use bullying tactics to get others to do as you wish? 0 1 2 3 4

32. Do you finish other people's sentences for them? 0 1 2 3 4

33. Do you get into physical fights with others, especially with strangers? 0 1 2 3 4

34. At family meals, do you control the conversation? 0 1 2 3 4

35. When you meet a stranger, are you the first to introduce yourself and begin a conversation? 0 1 2 3 4

Another tool that has been helpful to many individuals is taking the Myers-Briggs Type Indicator, a temperament assessment tool used by many professionals. Participating in taking the test, and attending a workshop where what is learned about yourself is applied in small groups of others of like temperament, can be a positive step in developing maturity in relationships with others. Myers-Briggs Type Indicator workshops not only assist in self-awareness but in understanding differences with others and ways to work through power conflicts arising from those differences. Contact a local psychologist to find out how you can take this test.

◇ 17 ◇

Step Nine: Ministering to Others

Step Nine: I am willing to be used by God as an instrument of healing and restoration in the lives of others.

Individuals who have been through traumatic experiences in their own lives often have a deep desire to help others who are hurting. This is a scriptural concept, as illustrated in 2 Corinthians 1, when Paul writes about comforting others with the comfort with which we have been comforted. This is a truly noble reason for ministry to others. Motivation for ministry can be very complex, however, and needs to be examined carefully.

Motivations for Ministry

Sometimes BECOMERS group members feel that ministry to others means that they *should* minister to sexual abuse victims. There are times, however, when individuals need to look at their motives as well as issues remaining in their own life that might interfere with true ministry.

When interviewing individuals for possible group leader positions, some have been very honest about their reasons for wanting to be involved with others who are in deep pain. These can include looking for a new challenge in life in the form of ministry, enhancing their self-worth, caretaking others because it feels good to see them dependent, desiring to have control over others, believing that good Christians should "do ministry" in order to please God. All these motives might be summed up as "giving to get." Most people-helpers have been motivated by one or more of these reasons on occasion. Ministry motivated by any reason will take time and energy, but ministry motivated by performance needs and "giving to get" will quickly tire a person out. Often this results in "burnout" or hurt, because those being ministered to are not responding with appropriate appreciation or change as a result of a person's effort to "minister" to them. Sadly, the end result of such self-effort is often disillusionment and giving up on helping others.

Unresolved Issues

While ministry can certainly occur before one has resolved all of the issues remaining in one's life, there needs to be an awareness of areas that might prove to be stumbling blocks in a ministry situation. For example, helpers might become hooked into a dependency relationship with someone they are trying to help. Often, the reason for this is the unresolved dependency issues in the helper.

Areas of sexual identity that remain unresolved might complicate ministry with victims of sexual abuse. Perhaps a same-sex relationship might ensue, or an opposite-sex attraction that could lead to a damaging relationship.

The helping person who has remaining inner conflicts toward parents or siblings may project those unresolved feelings onto those they are ministering to who have similar behavioral characteristics. An individual who had a passive mother who did not protect her from her father's sexual abuse may experience intense feelings in her interactions with passive members in a group setting. Individuals who have not resolved certain issues from their past—for example, forgiveness—will most likely have difficulty in encouraging others to deal with that issue. These types of "hooks" can be viewed as constructive signals illustrating unresolved issues that remain to be worked through. The presence of such "hooks" does not disqualify individuals from ministry, but they must be alert and aware of the potential for problems this could cause for themselves or others.

The Goal Is Love

The most healthy motive for ministering to others is found in 1 Tim. 1:5: "The goal . . . is love, which comes from a pure heart and a good conscience and a sincere faith." Because we cannot give away what we do not possess, ministry to others needs to come from experiencing God as the source of love before that love can be given away. Much ministry seems to be motivated by what could be called a "dirty" conscience—that is, by self-effort to perform for others or for God. The truth is that once receiving Christ, we have a pure heart in our standing before God. In His sight, each believer has free and open access to Him through Christ's finished work on the cross.

John 7:37 says, "If any man is thirsty, let him come to me and drink." To experience a pure heart and a clean conscience, thirsty Christians need to learn to rest, trust, and abide in Him as their source. Out of this relationship, Christ, in the person of the Holy Spirit, will flow out from the individual's heart to others as "rivers of living water." This work of the Spirit frees people to minister out of fullness, without expectations of, or "strings" attached to those to whom one is ministering.

"Baby Steps" to Ministry

Individuals can be encouraged to know that God can use them to minister in some way, whatever stage they may be in.

While the primary purpose of individuals involved in sexual abuse groups is to take care of themselves and focus on the work they need to do, they can also begin to minister to others by listening, offering feedback, or giving support. The advantage of "ministering" in such a setting will provide a measure of protection in a safe place. Feedback from group leaders and members can often help to clarify personal issues affecting the members' "ministry" to one another.

Marian was a group member who gave a great deal of feedback, usually in a parenting tone of voice, to anyone who shared. At first, group members felt intimidated by her. Eventually, the group was able to minister to Marian when they focused more on "speaking the truth in love" (Eph. 4:15) than worrying about what she would think about them if they told her the truth. Group members were able to help Marian see that her parenting style of trying to control them was interfering with her desire to be of honest help.

The importance of ministry is like being in a hostile, foreign country, needing safety. In that country, there is a small United States Embassy—not just a safe place, but actually American soil in the midst of hostile territory. The embassy can be compared to Christ, who is a safe place in the midst of this problem-plagued world. Persons who take refuge in Him are in a place of safety, and become His ambassadors. These ambassadors, then, are "safe" people for those to whom they minister. Just by being in the embassy, a citizen finds safety and rest.

Often, individuals who desire to help others feel inadequate to help. But being an "ambassador," a safe relationship for another, is a vital mission of the body of Christ, a ministry that can produce results every time they talk with someone on the phone or spend time with someone. Ministry may be difficult and draining, but it will not feel unbearable when God is its source.

The following poem describes one person's experience of ministry:

Ministry

Striving
　Obeying
　　Failing
　　　Growing
　　　　Quitting
Is ministry supposed to be so laborious, Lord?
　Did you intend it to be such a struggle?
　　Is there something lacking in me?
Weary
　Hurting
　　Fearing
　　　Inadequate
　　　　Ineffective
It is hard to call others to a life I struggle to
　live.
　　　　Where is the abundance, the joy, the peace?
　　　　Help me, Lord, to persevere.
Forgiven
　Learning
　　Changing

Helping
Sharing
It all makes up ministry, doesn't it, Father?
I desire to help others remove their pain,
but I forget to go to you with my own.
Loved
Adequate
Effective
Accepted
Challenged
I choose to believe all that you say, Lord.
You are sovereign over all.
I will persevere.
Yours . . . Anna[1]

A Ministry of Prevention

One specific ministry sexual abuse victims can have is to protect their own children, as well as other children, from sexual abuse. One preventive strategy is to insure that our children have a healthy self-esteem, but we will be unable to pass on a healthy sense of self to our children unless personal self-esteem issues are resolved. Shame is easily passed from one generation to the next. Without intervention, the chain will continue, leaving the child at risk.

A second principle of prevention is the development of active listening skills as a parent. Most victims have grown up in a family with poor communication skills where what they thought and felt was unimportant or overruled. Thus, their home was not a safe place in which to share either good or bad experiences. The confidence a child places in a parent as a good and "safe" listener is usually developed long before that child would first be approached by a child molester. It is the parents' responsibility to learn good communication skills and to teach those skills to their children.

A third area of prevention involves teaching "personal body safety" to children. Many adults who were victimized as children avoid talking about sexuality or sexual abuse to their chil-

---

[1]Anna Gates, 1986. Used by permission.

dren, which greatly increases the child's vulnerability to abusive situations. Children should be taught correct names for body parts and types of appropriate touch. Children need to be taught to be assertive in saying no if inappropriately approached or touched. Concerning obedience to authority, Christian parents need to be careful not to over-simplify the issue. Children should not be taught to "always obey their elders," but rather, they should be taught biblical examples of those who stood against authority when it was improperly used—Daniel, Esther, or the Apostle Peter. Parents also need to be educated in the signs and symptoms of abuse (see Chapter 3).

Fourth, teaching materials used to educate the child about sexuality in general and sexual abuse in particular will need to be repeated often to enhance the child's comprehension and retention. As children grow, their cognitive abilities will allow them to understand increasingly complex concepts about this very difficult issue. Too many parents have made the assumption that one session about sexual abuse is enough to equip their child.

After we have opened the door on this subject and taught sexual abuse preventive materials to our children, we should tell everyone in our circle of friends that we have done so. This will afford extra protection to the child by giving others permission to reinforce the parents' teaching. More importantly, it will alert anyone with whom the parents are acquainted that this child is not a "safe" victim, because he or she has been trained to refuse and report inappropriate touch.

Homework Questions

1. Who has been an instrument of restoration in my life?
2. Where have I seen healing in my life (in actions, character, responses, thoughts, interaction with others, etc.)?
3. Where do I think I still need to experience healing?
4. How could my past experiences enable me to encourage, accept, and bring healing or restoration to someone else?
5. Am I willing to be used in another person's life?

◇   ◇

Conclusion

The process of coming to healing from sexual abuse is not a random experience. While the program we present deals with many issues of sexual abuse in a sequence of somewhat progressive steps, healing will not be experienced in this way by most individuals. Many group members view their healing process as a spiral; they go over the same steps again and again, each time at a different level with new perspectives and insights.

The initial stages of the healing process often create an "emergency" in the victim's life. Dealing with repressed feelings brings havoc and results in constant crisis. Individuals fear they might "go crazy" or harm themselves. Even though this crisis time is difficult, it has a positive side as well: Crisis often drives a victim to seek help.

Many BECOMERS group members spend a year or two in intense individual and group counseling, then take a break from past abuse issues and focus on the present. In times of change, however—engagement, marriage, the birth of a child, the return to school—members may find unresolved memories and old feelings stirred up again. They take a "spiral" in their healing process. But the spiral is not regression. Rather, each spiral represents growth and offers victims an opportunity to strengthen their capacity to remember, to feel, to develop healthier relationships with God and others, and to make lasting changes in their lives.

Both for those who help and those who seek help, certain issues are of vital importance in the healing process. Women who were involved in an extensive BECOMERS research project prioritized the following issues. The items were rated in order of their significance in the women's recoveries, as well as reflecting which issues were considered most difficult. For example, forgiveness is a very important issue, but some of the other issues needed to be worked out first before the individual would be able to focus on forgiving or even understand its significance in his or her recovery. Issues in the process were:

1. Looking at the area of victimization.
2. Dealing with shame, guilt, and fear.
3. Honestly dealing with issues and taking responsibility for change.
4. Support of BECOMERS group and group leaders.
5. Individual therapy.
6. Sharing and letting go of feelings.
7. Looking to God as the source of help.
8. Dealing with issues of sexuality.
9. Forgiving self and/or the abuser.
10. Being used to help others.

Recovery from the ravages of sexual abuse is a process—for many, a lifelong struggle to face and deal with emotional and spiritual repercussions. A five- to ten-month treatment program is often only the beginning. But it is a beginning, and the progress achieved in that time gives hope for a future of normal, healthy relationships with God and others.

The individuals whose stories are told in this book are men and women of courage and integrity. They have allowed their pain and heartache to be revealed so that we might learn to help others like them. Too often, from lack of knowledge, God's people have been destroyed emotionally (Hos. 4:6). Unfortunately, we Christians have, in many cases, been guilty of trying to "heal their wounds lightly" (Jer. 6:14) out of ignorance about sexual abuse or an attempt to "fix" the problem.

Those who have suffered the trauma of sexual abuse deserve to receive help rather than condemnation. The principles presented here provide a framework for assisting abuse victims to come into freedom and wholeness. May we be obedient to the Word of God in Isa. 61:1, bringing *good news* to the suffering and afflicted, and comfort to the brokenhearted.

◇　◇

Appendix

This section offers a model to help others begin sexual abuse support groups. We have seen our own program adjusted to accommodate local situations and we urge others to adapt the program to fit their own needs and resources. Over the years, variations of BECOMERS have met diverse needs. Some programs have chosen a twenty-week format, combining a first week for introduction to the group, two weeks for each of the nine steps, and a final twentieth week for closure. Some groups bring in outside speakers each week; other groups every other week. Others have chosen to offer the program year-round, while others take several weeks off between sessions. Whatever the format, we ask that programs maintain the integrity of the BECOMERS ministry through guidelines outlined in the book, such as, requiring individual therapy for group members, providing "closed" groups to ensure trust-building, safety, and confidentiality, and using teaching materials and presenters that model God's redemptive and restorative grace, which empowers individuals to pursue their recovery process.

Our BECOMERS program involves a team approach including a professional director, trained group leaders, and a secretary. Local support from Christian therapists and pastors is an invaluable resource to the team. Modest funding for your program can be provided by charging BECOMERS group members a minimum fee for services provided. You may find yourself, as we did at first, without basic services available to you. If that is your situation, our recommendation is that you contact local churches, Christian social service agencies, Christian therapists in private practice, or local community centers to acquire a meeting place. We do not recommend meeting in a private home where it may prove difficult to maintain appropriate boundaries between group leaders and group members.

The Position of Director

The BECOMERS director should commit himself or herself to work for at least one year in his/her position. The director plans the program for each 9-week session, setting up topics to be covered and arranging for outside speakers or staff to teach on those issues. He or she should prepare the homework for each week, using materials suggested in this manual or by asking the speaker for the week to prepare the homework that will most benefit the group members.

The director also sets up training sessions for group leaders, facilitates support groups for these leaders, and is available for consultation and supervision of group leaders. It is the responsibility of the director to notify the therapist of concerns that arise within the context of a BECOMERS group and to consult with therapists about their clients should the need arise or at the request of the client. The director will need to take responsibility to acquire adequate consultation and supervision to enhance personal effectiveness in the role of director.

Director/Group Leader Qualifications

We would recommend that the director of any BECOMERS program have a degree in the field of human services, or a related field, and have a great deal of experience in sexual abuse counseling.

For both the director of the program and group leaders:

1. A leader needs to have a special desire or burden to work with sexual abuse victims, and a willingness to look at motivations for wanting to be involved. (See "Motivations for Ministry" in Chapter 17). If the leader has been a victim of sexual abuse, it would be imperative that personal issues be resolved through individual or group counseling. Once the BECOMERS group is established, new applicants for group leader positions who themselves have been victimized are requested to participate in the program as a group member for at least one nine-week session, or more if needed, to assess their readiness to

assume a leadership role. Sometimes, individuals have a real desire to work with abuse victims, but feel that they cannot do so because they themselves have not been abused. In our experience, this has had no bearing on one's ability to be an effective group leader. While such leaders may lack the natural empathy of shared experiences, they are often able to be more objective during group process. Whenever possible, BECOMERS groups function with two co-leaders in each group. It can be very effective to pair those who have been victimized with a partner who has not had that experience.

We suggest that directors and group leaders gain significant self-awareness not only about "hooks"[1] that might hinder their ministry, but also about their individual personality and the temperament type of those they will be working with. The Myers-Briggs Type Indicator is a helpful tool for this purpose. Group leader training sessions can further develop an understanding of and appreciation for personality differences among group leaders.

It is good for co-leaders to envision themselves in ministry together as Dr. Carl Whitaker and Dr. Augustus Napier viewed themselves in their work in *The Family Crucible*. They viewed themselves as the "parents" in the "family system" of their family therapy groups.[2]

As parents, group leaders must role-model healthy relationships and appropriate personal boundaries. Parents try to make their job obsolete. The more co-leaders understand and value themselves and others, the more effective they will be in their team ministry to those who have come from dysfunctional families.

2. It is important for the leader to have emotional stability, based on a solid self-image, rooted in Christ. This is needed to prevent the leader from "caretaking" the group members or from being dependent on group members for their self-esteem. To remain objective and equipped to minister to group members, leaders need the ability to rely on Christ as their source of strength in circumstances where group members project nega-

---

[1]For further insight see: Carmen R. Berry, *When Helping You Is Hurting Me: Escaping the Messiah Trap* (Harper and Row, 1988).

[2]Augustus Napier and Carl Whitaker, *The Family Crucible* (New York, N.Y.: Harper and Row, 1978).

tive feelings, strike out, challenge or condemn them.

3. Motivation and emotional stability need to be accompanied by knowledge about sexual abuse and skills in group process. These skills can be obtained through reading, attending specialized workshops, and by counseling experience. It is important that leaders have or acquire group leading skills—active listening as well as the ability to lead the group and facilitate sharing of feelings. One function of the group leader is to help provide a safe atmosphere for sharing, where group members feel protected and respected. A leader needs to have, or acquire, the ability to be very sensitive to the vulnerabilities of group members and be able to evaluate the level, and timing, of feedback and confrontation appropriate for group members.

An essential ingredient based on emotional stability is a willingness to learn from mistakes. Leaders will need to be able to openly receive feedback from other group leaders or group members.

4. The foundational ingredient for an effective group leader is spiritual maturity. This maturity will be evidenced in an everyday lifestyle that reflects Christian values and role models God's grace. It is especially important for a leader to unconditionally accept the spiritual condition of group members, being aware of and sensitive to the distortions of God that group members have experienced. Leaders need to exercise great care in applying scripture and prayer when meeting needs of group members.

5. Both the director and group leaders need to be committed to the program for at least one year to maintain continuity and to allow group members time to build trust. The director and group leaders will need regular meetings for support, evaluation, and consultation.

6. Both the director and group leaders need to be able to conduct intake interviews with new group members. The director or experienced group leader may include new group leaders in the interview process as a learning tool for new leaders. It can greatly enhance group experience for group members if they are then placed in the group with the leader who interviewed them. It is also advantageous to the BECOMERS group leader in giving them a great deal of background information

that may prove helpful in facilitating the group member's recovery.

7. A sample *Group Leader Application Form* is on p. 252.

BECOMERS Secretarial Duties

The BECOMERS secretary, the group's telephone contact person for the group, will need to have an understanding of the group's entry process and services which the group can and cannot provide.

Occasionally, BECOMERS groups get calls from persons who are victims of rape or domestic violence (i.e., wife battering). It will be important for the secretary to communicate that those needs are very valid and that the person should seek help, but that although the issues are similar to sexual abuse, there are enough significant differences that another referral would be more appropriate. It would be helpful to prepare a reputable reference list of related resources for such individuals.

The duties of the BECOMERS secretary/phone contact person are as follows:

1. In answering telephone calls, the BECOMERS secretary/ phone contact person will want to communicate as much of the following script as fits their group situation:

BECOMERS is designed as a one-year recovery program from the life experience of being sexually abused as a child or as an adolescent. We offer group counseling from a Christian perspective. The BECOMERS program is presented in three nine-week sessions per year. This does not mean that a group member must commit himself or herself to the program for the entire year. Conversely, a group member is not restricted to attending the program for only one year if that individual needs more time and is working through his/her healing process.

Each nine-week session focuses on different aspects of sexual abuse, so that none of the sessions are repeats of the one before or after it.

This year, our BECOMERS program will begin on (month, date) and end on (month, date). Meetings are from (time) on (day of week) at (name of location and address). Each group member is responsible for transportation to group.

Because BECOMERS must be a safe and confidential place to share, no one comes to "visit" and no one brings friends along. No new group members are brought into the groups after the first week of each session. New group members enter BECOMERS three times a year, at the beginning of each of the three sessions. For this year, new group members will be entering on the following dates:

Session One: (date)

Session Two: (date)

Session Three: (date)

Each group member is required to be in individual counseling at the same time that he or she is attending BECOMERS. The fees for individual counseling are arranged between the group member and the individual counselor.

Group members must have a professional referral from their counselor in order to enter the BECOMERS program. BECOMERS relies on professional counselors to determine the appropriateness of the BECOMERS program in meeting the individual needs of group members.

BECOMERS charges a small fee for each nine-week session that the group member attends. This fee is to cover printing costs for the homework materials and to provide honorarium fees for outside speakers.

Each group member commits to doing the assigned homework each week. This prepares group members to get the most benefit from the teaching time at the group session.

The group is structured into two parts. The first 30 to 45 minutes of group time is a teaching time where one of our psychologists, or staff persons, will present a topic relevant to sexual abuse. The week prior to that topic, group members will have homework to complete to increase their self-awareness of how that issue is affecting their life. The group member comes to group meetings, attends the large group teaching time, then goes into a small group for a support/application/discussion time for the next hour or hour and a half.

Each small group has no more than eight group members, and is facilitated by a group leader or co-leaders. The group member remains in the same small group with the same group leader/s for the entire nine-week session.

At the end of the nine-week session, new clients will be

added to the group to fill vacancies of those who have "graduated" themselves.

When entering the BECOMERS program, each group member makes a commitment to attend for that entire nine-week session. At the end of that nine-week session, group members have the option to continue on, to drop out, or to "graduate" themselves from the program. Almost all clients choose to continue for at least one year, but they recommit themselves nine weeks at a time.

2. In addition to telephone contacts, the BECOMERS secretary may have to explain and follow group members through the group entry process.

The Entry Process

- Initial contact with BECOMERS phone contact person.
- If prospective group member is already in therapy, he is sent a *Consent for Release of Information* form (see sample on p. 255) to sign and return to the BECOMERS secretary, giving written permission to the group to contact his/her therapist for a referral.
- The release form and the *Professional Referral Form* (see sample on p. 256) are then sent to the therapist.
- After the therapist has returned the referral form, the applicant is scheduled for an intake interview with the director or another experienced group leader.
- After completing the interview, the applicant completes a *BECOMERS Group Member Application Form*, which is kept on file for use in contacting family members or close friends in case of emergency.
- The new group member then enters the actual BECOMERS group at the next available opening.
- If, at the initial contact, the person is *not* in individual counseling, encourage him/her to contact a professional known to BECOMERS or some other counseling resource for a referral and to begin the group entry process as listed above.

---

3. Send out release of information forms. In order for a BECOMERS staff person or the BECOMERS program director to consult with the group member's counselor, or for the therapist to be able to fill out a referral form for BECOMERS, a *Consent*

for Release of Information Form must be signed by the prospective group member. Make a copy for each group member's file.

4. Prepare master list of BECOMERS group members in alphabetical order. This is for the director's use. Update list each nine weeks when group members change.

5. Make up interview packets for group member interviews. Interview packets contain the following forms:

Intake Interview Outline Form (see sample on p. 258)

Group Member Application Form (see sample on p. 261)

"Ground Rules" for BECOMERS (see sample on p. 263)

BECOMERS Commitment Form (see sample on p. 265)

BECOMERS Brochure (see sample on p. 266)

6. Keep a file for each group member. This file will include: a copy of the release of information form, the interview outline, the group application form, commitment form, and any correspondence with the counselor of the group member.

7. Compile a list of Christian counselors and therapists with expertise in the area of sexual abuse. This list can be sent upon request to prospective group members who do not yet have an individual counselor. Such a support team of professionals is invaluable for consultation and supervision.

8. Contact prospective group members for intake interviews. To complete the BECOMERS group entry process, each group member is interviewed by the director or one of the group leaders. The purpose of this interview is to allow the group member to have individual contact with one staff person prior to entering the group. This will allow the staff person to get a history from the group member about their abuse situation, and to evaluate the appropriateness of this prospective group member for the BECOMERS program. This interview, which lasts about an hour to an hour and a half, will provide a supportive environment in which the group member can share on a one-to-one basis. Meeting for this interview may also help the prospective group member feel more comfortable at the first group session.

9. Group members may fill out a group evaluation form at the end of each nine-week session. This feedback is very valuable in assessing how the group process is being perceived by the group members, and to evaluate their individual progress. This is also a tool for evaluating the effectiveness of group leaders (See sample *Group Member Evaluation Form* on p. 270.)

Group Leader Application for BECOMERS Ministry
(Sample Form)

Name: _____ Date: _____

Address: _____

_____

Phone: (home) _____ (work) _____

Birthdate: _____ Occupation: _____

Church affiliation: _____

Please list any involvement/s you may have at your church:

_____

_____

Involved in other groups? _____

_____

_____

Previous counseling experience (if any): _____

_____

_____

Have you ever been in counseling? If so, write about what that
experience was like for you: _____

_____

_____

Is your spouse supportive of your becoming involved with
BECOMERS? _____

_____

What do you see as priorities in your life? How will those priorities be affected by your becoming a group leader in BECOMERS?

_____

_____

_____

_____

_____

_____

Describe your personal relationship with Jesus Christ: _____

_____

_____

_____

_____

What spiritual gifts are you aware of in your life? _____

_____

_____

How do you feel that God has called you specifically to the BECOMERS ministry? _____

_____

_____

_____

_____

Describe your personal understanding of how God wants to work in the life of someone who is coping with the experience of childhood sexual abuse: _____

_____

_____

_____

_____

If you have been a victim of any type of abuse, describe some of your personal healing process, and what things/experiences/ people have been helpful to you in your healing process:

_____

_____

_____

_____

_____

What do you consider your personal strengths? _____

_____

_____

_____

What do you consider your personal weaknesses? _____

_____

_____

_____

References:

Previous therapist (if any): _____

Address: _____

_____

Character reference: (name) _____

Address: _____

_____

Character reference: (name) _____

Address: _____

_____

Consent for Release of Information Form
(Sample Release Form)

I consent to the release of private information about me to the agency or individual named below. I understand I may revoke this consent at any time, not retroactive, and that upon accomplishment of the requested release, this consent will expire. In any event, this consent will expire one year from the date of my signature.

Group member's therapist:

Name: _____

Address: _____

_____

Agency or individual to whom information will be released:

(Your Becomer's Group)

Name: _____

Address: _____

_____

☐ Referred into Becomer's Group

☐ Consultation

This information is to be used for the following purpose: to enhance individual therapy with group experience relating to issues of sexual abuse.

Group Member's Signature: _____

Date: _____

Signature of Parent or Guardian (if under 18): _____

Witness (if necessary): _____

Professional Referral Form
Sexual Abuse Support Group Referral
(Sample referral form to be completed by group member's therapist)

Based on the MMPI and/or clinical interview you have had with

_____ are you aware of any

psychological problems that may prohibit the client from functioning effectively within the group setting?

- psychotic disorder   YES ☐   NO ☐
- suicidal behaviors   YES ☐   NO ☐
- extremely manipulative behaviors   YES ☐   NO ☐
- other _____

Do you feel the client could benefit from participation in a support group for victims of sexual abuse?   YES ☐   NO ☐
If not, please explain: _____

_____

What is your evaluation of this client's group compatibility?

_____

_____

_____

- commitment to Christ and/or openness to Biblical approaches to problem solving   YES ☐   NO ☐
- any indication of an emerging desire for wellness

                                     YES ☐   NO ☐
- client able to verbalize experience of sexual abuse at least to some degree   YES ☐   NO ☐

Any further comments: _____

_____

_____

Specific needs/goals of this client: _____

_____

_____

Will you be seeing this client on an individual basis?

YES ☐   NO ☐

Thank you,

Signature: _____

Date: _____

Intake Interview Outline Form

(Sample form to be used by interviewer)

Name: _____ Date: _____

Interviewed by _____

A word or phrase to describe "mother." _____

_____

How did she express love to you? _____

_____

How did she express feelings? i.e., anger, fear, sadness. _____

What "messages" did you get from her? How do you think she

felt about you? _____

_____

A word or phrase to describe "father." _____

_____

How did he express love to you? _____

_____

How did he express feelings to you? i.e., anger, fear, sadness.

_____

_____

What "messages" did you get from him? How do you think he

felt about you? _____

_____

How did your parents express love/care to each other? _____

_____

How did your parents express feelings to each other? i.e., anger,

sadness, fear. _____

How do you express feelings? Repress/strike out/talk out/etc.

_____

_____

How do you express love? (to spouse/kids/others) _____

_____

Do you have some thoughts about which feelings are okay to have and which feelings are not okay? _____

_____

What was your placement in the family? Siblings? (Diagram client's family placement.)

Relationships with siblings? _____

_____

Who was the initial sexual abuse offender? _____

Your age at the time? _____

When it began/how long? _____

Specific incidents/sources of pain. _____

How do you feel about offender/self/parents? _____

_____

Did you tell anyone? Their response was: _____

_____

Have others sexually or physically abused you? If so, who?

_____

_____

How have you "survived" thus far—coping skills/relationships?

_____

_____

Have you used drugs or alcohol to help you cope? _____

Have you had inpatient treatment for chemical use or psychological problems? _____

How has the sexual abuse affected your sexuality? (Have you
been involved in a sexual relation with persons of the same sex?)

_____

_____

What is your relationship to your spouse/boyfriend/lover? ____

_____

Have you been in any other groups? _____

How did you hear about the BECOMERS program? _____

_____

Interviewer then explains group structure/location/fees, etc.

BECOMERS
Group Member Application Form
(Sample Form)

Name: _____

Birthdate: _____

Address: _____

_____

Phone: _____

Referred By: _____

Family Information:

    Marital Status: _____

    Spouse: _____

    Children: _____

    _____

    Other: _____

    _____

Educational Background: _____

_____

Employment: _____

Church Background: _____

Previous Therapy: _____

_____

Current Medication: _____

Describe any chemical use: _____

_____

Describe current family situation: _____

_____

Name and emergency phone number of closest family member:

_____

_____

Name and emergency phone number of closest friend: _____

_____

What you would most like to gain from being involved in the BECOMERS sexual assault support group: _____

_____

_____

"Ground Rules" for BECOMERS

(Sample Group Rules)

The following guidelines have been found helpful in groups. They are an informal kind of "constitution." The closer we all follow them, the better the experience will be for all.

1. Everyone Who Is Here Belongs Here.

- No one can change this rule except the group leader.
- If everyone in the group is unhappy with one person, this does not change his or her *belonging in it.*
- If a person withdraws him or herself from the group, this does not change their belonging in it.
- If a person gives up on themselves, the group does not give up on them.
- If a group member is unfair to everyone, the group says so and tries to help with the problem.
- If a person has a problem that appears "hopeless," the group keeps them company with it.

2. It Is Everyone's Responsibility to Tune-in and Talk-up.

- Without this rule, the group is just a collection of people without purpose.
- *Tuning-in* means:
  1. You listen to someone's words.
  2. You are sensitive to the feelings they express verbally and non-verbally.
  3. You pay attention to your own reactions as the other person is communicating.
- *Talking-up* means you give *feedback.*
  1. You check out with them what you "thought" they were saying or doing.
  2. You share your response to it.
- Tuning-in and talking-up must go together.
- This does not come easy for some people, but we all can learn.
- We can all have different "feelings" about the same "fact."

- People change and perceptions change . . . if we allow it.
- Confrontation in the group will focus on negative thoughts/behaviors, if necessary, but the value of each person will not be questioned.

3. Everyone Is Ultimately Responsible for Their Own Behavior.

- This is the only way to handle "Who's responsible?"
- No one is forced to say anything. Sometimes we need encouragement to try new things, but we have the right to say "no."

4. What We Say and Do in the Group Belongs Only to the Group.

- Honest expression is not so much the telling of private facts; it is the *revealing* of what we feel and are as persons. Therefore, personal sharing will focus on thought patterns, "messages" and feelings resulting from sexual abuse, rather than on the detailed exclosure of actual physical events of the abuse.
- We can "know" one another without knowing many things "about" one another.
- If someone wants something shared outside of the group about themselves, it is their responsibility alone to share it.
- If we have feelings of distrust, it is important that they be faced if we are to grow. Doing nothing does not reflect growth or learning.

Adapted from Dr. Carl Haugen.

BECOMERS Commitment Form

(Sample Form)

In joining the BECOMERS support group, I understand:

1. That my regular attendance and prompt arrival is expected and I commit myself to the entire nine-week cycle.

2. That if I am unable to attend a session, I will notify my group leader.

3. That if I am absent from two consecutive weekly sessions without contacting my group leader, I will be asked to withdraw from that nine-week session.

4. That the purpose of the support group is not to gain head knowledge only, but rather apply and experience God's truth in my own life.

5. That I will do the homework each week because I need the comfort, insight, and confronting that it gives me as I seek God's will and His help in my recovery.

6. That an essential part of my healing will come from individual work with a private therapist and that I will participate in individual counseling while I am involved with BECOMERS.

7. That my fee is enclosed for the next nine-week session.

I agree to commit myself to these principles for the _____ session of the BECOMERS program, _____ .

Signed: _____ Date: _____

An introduction to

. . . a support group
to promote emotional and spiritual healing
from the life experience of childhood sexual abuse.

Who can participate in a BECOMERS Support Group?

Any adolescent or adult male or female who . . .

★ is hesitant to identify himself or herself as a victim of sexual abuse

★ feels isolated, depressed, worthless, shameful, helpless to change

★ is struggling with feelings about God in relation to his or her life experience of being sexually abused

★ condemns himself or herself, trying to deny that being abused in the past somehow affects present circumstances

★ feels out of control, defeated in areas of compulsive behaviors

★ feels angry, bitter, rebellious, having trouble with authority figures

★ preoccupied with thoughts about having a "normal" relationship with the opposite sex

★ questions his or her sexual identity and/or is experiencing confusion regarding his or her own sexuality

★ questions self-reality · "Who am I?"

★ is desiring to have victory through Christ over the life experience of sexual abuse

and

★ is willing to participate in individual counseling with a professional therapist who is supportive of Christian faith and values

We are called BECOMERS because . . .

". . . Now we are children of God, and what we will become has not yet been made known. But we know that when he appears, we shall be like him, for we shall see him as he is."
— *I John 3:2 (NIV)*

The objectives of BECOMERS are:

1. to provide a safe and accepting atmosphere in which to share feelings and explore doubts related to childhood sexual abuse.

2. to offer a one year recovery program, presented in three 9-week sessions. Each 9-week session will focus on different aspects of sexual abuse.

3. to provide materials which will encourage group members to actively participate with God in the healing of their damaged emotions and in recognizing and challenging negative thought patterns.

4. to establish a group support system which can be helpful in building constructive interpersonal relationships as a pattern to enhance the experience of becoming whole in Christ.

5. to be an adjunct to, not a replacement for, professional individual counseling.

Each group member will:

- participate in a personal inventory evaluation with a therapist followed by an intake interview with a **BECOMERS** staff person, prior to entering the group.

- see an individual therapist concurrently with participation in **BECOMERS.**

- make an initial commitment to **BECOMERS** to regularly attend each meeting with the option to continue or terminate at the end of each 9-week session.

- keep a journal and/or participate in homework for personal growth.

- be assured of a confidential and safe atmosphere in the group.

BECOMERS Covenant of Confidentiality

1. Only group members who have completed the intake process will attend BECOMERS meetings.

2. No new group members will enter any given 9-week cycle after week #2.

3. Each individual support group will have a group facilitator and no more than 8 group members.

4. No information about group members will be shared within the group, or outside the group, unless permission is given by the individual group member for a specific purpose.

5. Personal sharing will focus on thought patterns and feelings resulting from sexual abuse rather than on the detailed disclosure of actual events of the sexual abuse.

For further information, contact:

(Place local BECOMERS group contact address here)

Please specify whether your request is for services to male victims or female victims.

All services of the **BECOMERS** support group are confidential. Each group participant will be requested to pay a minimal fee prior to beginning each 9-week session to cover homework materials and printing costs.

Group Member Evaluation Form
(Sample Form)

Please complete and bring to the group with you on the final meeting of the 9-week session.

Name _____

1. What were some of your expectations about the past 9-week session of BECOMERS? _____

_____

2. What happened that you expected to happen? _____

_____

_____

3. What happened that you did not expect to happen? _____

_____

_____

4. What is an area in which you have seen progress in the past 9 weeks? _____

_____

5. Write about your feelings of belonging, or of not belonging, in your group. _____

_____

6. What is the area you are most struggling with at this time?

_____

_____

7. How has/hasn't the group supported you in that struggle?

_____

_____

BECOMERS Client Evaluation Form
(Sample Form B)

Client Name: _____

Name of group facilitator: _____

Session attended (date and year): _____

Respond in brief statements, regarding your evaluation of (1)Is this an issue for you? (2)Was it processed in group? (3)Is there more work to be done? in each of the following areas:

1. Powerlessness _____

2. Healing process / Hope for the future _____

3. Shame / guilt _____

4. Identity / self-esteem _____

5. Sharing feelings, such as anger, grieving losses, fear, pain

    _____

6. Experience of repeated victimization / present-day responses _____

7. Forgiveness _____

8. Maturing / growing in relationship with God, spouse, significant others _____

9. Readiness to be "helper" _____

Boundaries _____

Describe areas where you have seen significant progress.

Discuss any current areas of concern you have.

How would you summarize your healing process during this session?

Note: If client did not complete session, please explain.

Index